A Western Horseman Book

Colorado Springs, Colorado

WESTERN HORSEMANSHIP

By Richard Shrake

with Pat Close

Photographs by Darrell Arnold

WESTERN HORSEMANSHIP

Published by
The Western Horseman, Inc.

3850 North Nevada Avenue
P.O. Box 7980
Colorado Springs, Colorado 80933

Typography and Production
Western Horseman
Colorado Springs, Colorado

Printing
Williams Printing
Colorado Springs, Colorado

Design
Dwayne Brech

ISBN 0-911647-09-0

DEDICATION

This book is dedicated to the many students and horsemen, young and old, who have given me the privilege to share with them their love for horses . . . and to be a part of their dreams, whether they only learn to feel and communicate with their horses or go on to win world championships.

Richard Shrake

RICHARD SHRAKE

On the cover: Richard Shrake and his stepdaughter, Jill.

CONTENTS

1 INTRODUCTION

Horsemanship is more than correct position in the saddle.

Horsemanship, in its simplest definition, is the art of riding a horse. A good rider is not only one who has complete control of his horse, but one who never hinders the movement of the horse. Both rider and horse work together as one, in total harmony.

For this reason, horsemanship is more than correct position in the saddle. It is, perhaps above all else, a soft and subtle communication between rider and horse. The horse knows what the rider is asking through the subtlest of cues. The rider, in turn, feels what the horse is communicating through his mouth and body.

Good horsemanship helps cutting horse riders stay in synch with their horses. Showing excellent balance is John Tolbert, riding Boons Sierra.
Photo courtesy National Cutting Horse Association.

As hotly competitive as barrel racing is, good horsemanship is a prime requisite. This is Bill Cochran making a tight turn on I Haul It Too, owned by Max Gibson of Terre Haute, Indiana.
Photo by Harold Campton

Not too many years ago, we used to judge horsemanship, or equitation as it is also called, primarily by the way a youngster sat in the saddle. If his (or her) hand was exactly one inch above the horse, his eyes never looked down, his back was perfectly straight, and his legs never moved out of position, he was a star and won it all. But now horsemanship has become more sophisticated, and in practically all horsemanship classes, riders are asked to do tests to see if they can really handle their horses . . . to communicate with them. A rider must be able to ride in rhythm with the horse, to balance him, and to soften him if he becomes too stiff. Whatever a test might require, the horse and rider must be able to execute everything well, with no heavy-handedness or roughness by the rider, and no head-fighting, stiffness, or resistance by the horse.

Although a rider must have soft hands, this doesn't mean hands that

If a roper can't stay in balance and rhythm with his horse, it can cost him time—and money. Mike Craig, Elbert, Colo., has everything under control for heeler Jack Wright of Canon City, Colo., to make his throw.

never move. If the horse is running off with you, and you're pulling with one pound of pressure, that won't stop him. But if he's working properly, is really light, and you pick him up with 20 pounds of pressure and smack his mouth, his head will fly up and his mouth will open. That will cost you points.

No matter in which events you like to compete, improved horsemanship techniques can help you do a better job of showing your horse, and that, in turn, will improve your chances of winning. If a cutting horse rider, for example, is out of synch with his horse, he's hindering that horse. If a roper can't stay in balance with his horse, it can cost him time,

and in this day and age, one-tenth of a second can be the difference between $5,000 and feathers.

You would not think western pleasure riders would have to be good jockeys just to ride around on the rail. But they've got to understand rhythm, balance, collection, and cadence.

Look at some of the top reining horse riders. You might not think their position is absolutely correct, in terms of what is considered correct in a horsemanship class. But believe me, they understand how a horse moves, when he might be dropping a shoulder, and how to keep him balanced and pretty in his circles, run-downs, and stops. And they understand that you stop a horse with finesse,

Even pleasure riders will benefit from improving their horsemanship. These riders are enjoying the scenery in the Monument Valley Navajo Tribal Park, located on the Utah/Arizona border.

and that's why you don't often see their horses resist in the poll or mouth.

Barrel racers understand that letting their weight shift incorrectly toward the barrel can kick the horse's rear end out. This, in turn, causes him to drop his inside shoulder and probably knock the barrel over.

Even weekend pleasure riders will benefit from working to improve their horsemanship. They will enjoy riding more, they will have better control of their horses, and they can more easily cope with such situations as a stubborn horse that refuses to cross water.

It also goes without saying that horses who are ridden by good riders certainly enjoy being used . . . more so than horses subjected to heavy-handed riders who continually bounce in the saddle.

No matter what your goal may be as a rider, the purpose of this book is to help you become a better horseman which, in turn, will help your horses become better performers.

No matter what your specialty may be in the show ring, good horsemanship is a must if you expect to bring some trophies and ribbons home. This is Angie Ross of Aurora, Colo., riding Casa String.

9

2 SELECTING THE HORSE

If you mismatch disposition of horse and rider, you're in trouble.

As far as I'm concerned, attitude and disposition are the two most important factors in finding the right horse for a rider. I'll tell you what . . . if you mismatch disposition of horse and rider, you're in trouble.

For example, suppose I have a rider who is extremely hyperactive, quick moving, or aggressive. If I put him, or her, on a nervous horse, I'll have a wreck on my hands. But if I take that rider and put him on a horse that's a little laid back, and maybe even on the lazy side,

that will make a nice blend of the two dispositions.

On the other hand, if I have rider who is extremely mild-mannered and passive and put him on the same type of horse, he will never get anything done. It's very difficult for a passive rider to bring a lot out of a lazy horse. This rider needs a horse that is fairly sensitive and responsive. If the horse is a little nervous, the calmness of the rider usually serves to quiet the horse.

I've never had an aggressive rider

Kelly Holder of Bend, Ore., and her Arabian, El Baraka, show a good match-up of horse and rider. Kelly's size does not overpower the horse, yet she isn't too small for him either. Note that her legs do not hang below the horse's girth.

10

PARTS OF THE HORSE

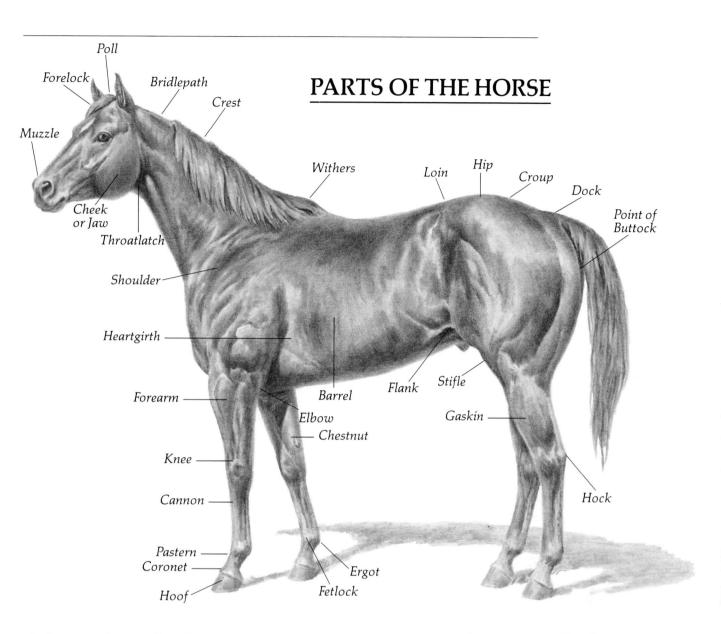

who's gotten along well with a sensitive horse, nor have I had a passive rider who's done well with a laid-back horse. And here, I'm talking about top riders in major shows.

There are also other factors I look for. The horse should be pretty, if at all possible. Even though the rules say only the rider is being judged, a judge cannot help but be influenced by the overall picture of the horse and rider. If together they make a pretty picture, the judge will be impressed.

The horse should also be well made, although he doesn't need to be a halter champion, and he should be a pretty mover with soft, fluid gaits. If he's got a rough jog or lope, the rider will have a tough time sitting the saddle properly.

In looking at a horse, I always like to see the top line of the neck (from the withers to the poll) longer than the bottom line (from the throatlatch to the chest). This allows the horse to flex more easily for a better headset, and also gives him more balance.

I also like to see the top line of the neck longer than the line that goes from the withers to the imaginary line from one hip bone to the other, across the rump. In all my experience with horses, I've never seen a horse that was a good mover when his back line was longer than the line from the withers to the poll.

Since so many of today's horsemanship classes require individual work such as stops, spins, and figure-eights with flying changes, the horse must also have some athletic ability. He should be fairly well trained, with a good headset and mouth. If a horse gaps at the mouth and throws his head whenever the rider takes

This illustration is based on the American Quarter Horse Association's ideal Quarter Horse, as painted by Orren Mixer.

11

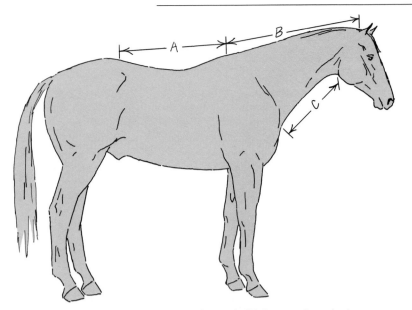

I always like to see the top line of the neck (B) longer than the bottom line (C), and also longer than the line that goes from the withers to the hips (A).

up on the reins, it reflects poor horse-manship.

Matching the size of the horse to the rider is also important. In fact, I used to think it was the most important factor, but no more. Still, you don't want a 6'2" boy on a 14-2 horse. Sometimes when I can't find a tall-enough horse for a rider, I can go with a longer-bodied horse that's maybe not as tall as I'd like him. The length of the horse gives more balance to the overall picture of the horse and rider . . . the rider doesn't seem quite as tall as he really is, and is more in proportion to the horse.

By the same token, if I have a really tall horse that is short-backed and short-coupled, I can sometimes match a shorter rider to that horse—a rider who would ordinarily need a shorter horse.

One thing you never want is a rider's legs hanging seven or eight inches below the horse's girth. If I have a really long-legged rider, sometimes I can put him on a horse only 15 hands, but who's thick through the heartgirth and barrel, and that helps take care of the problem.

Ideally, though, you want a horse that's a little flat-sided so the rider's legs can hang as straight as possible. It's tough for a short-legged youngster on a big-barreled horse to ride with his legs in the correct position.

Going back to disposition, the horse shouldn't have a cranky, sour attitude. If he pins his ears and swishes his tail all the time, the judge might think the rider is miscueing the horse; he won't realize it's simply the horse's normal attitude.

You can check for this by walking up to a horse and touching his side, or pinching his shoulder. If he pins his ears and is irritated, you can bet he'll do it under saddle and in the show ring.

When trying out a horse, be sure and ride him where there's lots of activity going on. Check to see if his mind wanders off to watch the other activities, or if he pays attention to you.

If there is a group of riders present, see if you can ride the horse away from the other horses. He should leave willingly. In the arena or ring, he should stay on the rail, even though there may be other horses in the middle of the arena. Likewise, you should be able to take him off the rail and do individual maneuvers in the center of the arena.

It's not unusual to see a horse whose rider cannot keep him on the rail by himself, or a horse that's been ridden on the rail so much, he's lost if he gets off it.

The color of a horse has no relevance in a horsemanship class, but I will say that a horse with a crooked blaze might be a problem. That's because it might give the judge the impression that the horse is carrying his head crooked.

Sometimes an otherwise good horse carries a crooked tail. Although it can detract from an overall pretty picture, I wouldn't worry about it. But you do not want a horse that tends to wring or pop his tail every time a fly lands on him or the rider cues him.

Sometimes youngsters who show in open horsemanship classes have a problem if they are riding Arabs or Morgans when the predominant horses in the classes are Quarter Horses, Paints, or Appaloosas. This is especially true if the judge tends to be a Quarter Horse-type person, because he is not familiar with the different style with which other breeds are usually ridden.

I believe, however, that more judges of today who are primarily associated with one breed are keeping more of an open mind when they judge classes or events open to all breeds. They are beginning to realize that there are good working horses in all breeds.

I personally feel that if a youngster on, say, an Arab, follows good horsemanship principles with quiet hands, a secure seat, organized legs, and a real feel on the horse, he will be competitive. I also feel that the natural balance of most Arabians can really be an advantage to horsemanship riders.

On the other hand, if a youngster is not a good rider—he can't get his horse to move in balance, and the horse is always resisting him—he's not going to do well no matter what breed of horse he is riding. Likewise, if his horse is not trained well enough for competition. For example, being able to take both leads correctly is one of the most basic requirements, but it's surprising how many horses will not readily do this.

One thing I've found is that young riders always match up better with cute horses having big, expressive eyes with little fox ears. This is Melissa Coffey of Scappoose, Oregon.

13

3 THE OVERALL LOOK

You should project the image of a perfect rider.

I would like to mention the importance of the overall look you should present as a rider, because your appearance can really help you or hinder you. Your goal is to project the image of a perfect rider. As an analogy, I often use this example:

Suppose you are sitting in the dentist's chair, waiting for him to come in. Suddenly he appears—wearing jogging shorts, a wild plaid shirt, sunglasses, and carrying a Walkman blaring rock music. You would probably get up and run, because his appearance gives you no confidence that he knows anything about dentistry.

It's the same way in the show ring. Your appearance should immediately make the judge think, "Hey, that rider looks like he knows how to do something on a horse. He must be a good hand."

Angie Ross shows a good overall position and a neat workmanlike outfit, sure to catch the eye of any judge.

Creating a good impression as soon as you enter the show ring is the first step to winning. This well-turned-out rider is Melissa Mitsch, who won the national championship in stock seat equitation at the 1985 U.S. Arabian Nationals. Melissa is from Rogers, Minn., was 15, and was riding 19-year-old Chasqui Del Viento. **Photo by Rob Hess**

The image you create as a rider is influenced partially by your horse, gear, and apparel, and these topics are covered in other chapters. But it's primarily determined by your position on a horse and how well you ride.

A pretty rider is one who has the ability to sit tall while relaxed. We don't want a stiff rider, one who looks like he will topple over if the horse makes the slightest bobble. Your eyes, as well as your entire appearance, should reflect confidence. Your hands, feet, and legs should be steady.

You should be sitting in the middle of the horse, and sitting square, not on one hip or the other. And you should have that look of being able to move with that horse in perfect balance with him; you should *flow* with his movements, and not resist him.

The photos on these two pages are of Shannon Baker, Glendale, California. Her outfit typifies the popular look of equitation riders in California. In 1985 Shannon won the reserve championship in the AHSA stock seat medal finals held at the Cow Palace in San Francisco.
Photos by Steve White

The judge looks for the rider with cadence and balance with his horse.

The overall look is so important because it's the first impression a judge gets as riders enter the ring. He's looking for riders who look like good hands, who are quiet, and who are communicating with their horses. As you enter the ring, if you are resisting the motion of your horse and he's fighting his head, or if he's not staying steady in his gait, you've lost the class before you've even begun.

As riders begin to work on the rail, the judge is looking for the rider with cadence and balance with his horse, whose eyes are up and looking where he's going. His shoulders are square, his back is

flat, his hands are quiet, and he reflects a proud look.

I cannot emphasize enough the importance of first impressions at the major shows where judges must work large classes as quickly as possible. One year when I was a judge at the All American Quarter Horse Congress in Ohio, I had 118 riders in one horsemanship class and was told by show management that I had 45 minutes to judge the class. In a situation like that, no judge has time to analyze each rider and tally up points. The judge must make rapid decisions, and a lot of it is based on first impressions.

In this case, riders came into the ring in sections. Based on a simple, short individual test, I picked the top riders in each section and then had them come back for the rail work. My decision as to which riders I picked for my final placings was partially influenced by their appearance and overall look.

So learn to sit correctly, have the right equipment, dress properly, and develop a confident attitude . . . the look of an eagle, the look of a rider sitting tall in the saddle.

4 EQUIPMENT

You can tell a lot about a rider just by his appearance and equipment.

Here are two good-looking, workmanlike saddles ideal for horsemanship classes. They have nice tooling and just enough silver to make them attractive, not gaudy. The suede seats help the rider stick tighter; the horns (especially the one on the right) are fairly low so they will not interfere with the rein hand; and the stirrups are hung properly so the rider can keep his legs under him. I personally feel that a single skirt is a little neater for horsemanship, and I like in-skirt rigging because it creates less bulk under the rider's legs. The saddle on the right has a much better stirrup for horsemanship because it's wider and gives the rider more use of the ball of his foot.

Anybody who has been around horses for a reasonable amount of time knows that you can tell a lot about a rider just by his appearance and equipment. In fact, you can tell how good a hand a person might be just by his actions around a horse—how he halters and leads him, how he brushes him, by the way he takes care of his equipment, and even by the way he talks. If he hangs his bridle upside down or backwards, or says such things as "I've just had my horse shoed," it's a dead giveaway that he's a novice in the horse world.

Arnold "Chief" Rojas is one of the last of the old-time vaqueros in California. He tells stories about the old days when a vaquero or cowboy would ride into a ranch, perhaps looking for a job, perhaps just for a meal. No matter which, he never had to say a word about where he was from, or how good a hand he was. The foreman could tell just by listening to him talk, and looking at his

PARTS OF THE SADDLE

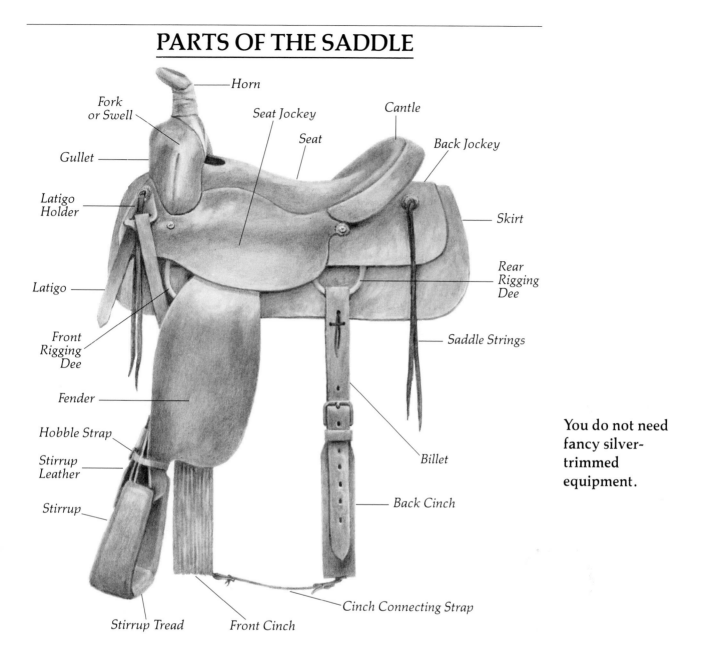

Horn

Fork or Swell

Seat Jockey

Cantle

Seat

Back Jockey

Gullet

Skirt

Latigo Holder

Rear Rigging Dee

Latigo

Saddle Strings

Front Rigging Dee

Fender

Billet

Hobble Strap

Stirrup Leather

Back Cinch

Stirrup

Cinch Connecting Strap

Stirrup Tread

Front Cinch

You do not need fancy silver-trimmed equipment.

equipment and what he wore.

That's the way it is in the show ring today, although it is more difficult to identify where a rider is from than it was in years past. In those days, it was easy to tell if riders were from the West Coast, Texas, the Midwest, or the East by their equipment and clothes. But today, styles have intermingled, and someone you think might be from California could be from Illinois.

But a judge who is a long-time horseman can tell if a rider is a top hand or what I call a "vanilla competitor" by his saddle and other gear. This doesn't necessarily mean fancy, silver-trimmed equipment. What it does mean is equipment that is neat, clean, and workmanlike—and the key phrase is workmanlike.

Saddles are very much a matter of personal preference, but one for the

BROWBAND HEADSTALL

A browband bridle with silver buckles and conchas.

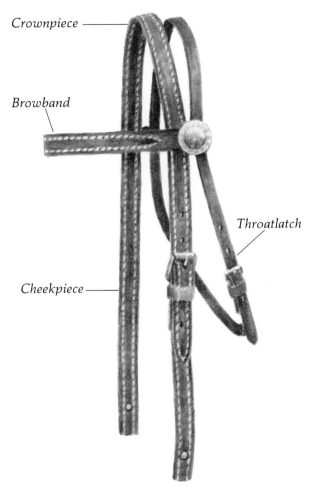

Crownpiece

Browband

Throatlatch

Cheekpiece

show ring should look as if you could do a day's job in it on the ranch. I realize saddles are expensive, but try to get the best one you can. One that looks as if it is made of cardboard and held together by staples will not enhance your image in the eyes of the judge.

Even more important: the saddle should fit both rider and horse, and this can be a problem with small children. Sometimes they have to ride hand-me-down saddles that are too big for them. On the other hand, if you get a small saddle to fit the child, sometimes it won't fit the horse properly. Some kids' saddles

are made with no thought given to the fact they will go on full-size horses.

Saddles can make or break a rider. Unfortunately, there is no correlation between the looks of a saddle and how well it rides. If the seat has been made poorly, or the stirrups hung too far forward or back, trying to ride it correctly is an uphill battle. Some saddles are also made with such thick leather it's difficult to have any feel of the horse under you—especially if the latigo secures right under your leg.

Since most saddles are designed with men in mind, they are sometimes too

ONE-EAR HEADSTALL

A neat, split-ear headstall.

wide for girls and women. This makes them uncomfortable.

In the 1960s and '70s, many equitation saddles were made with a deep seat that was built up in front. This helped the rider stay in the correct position because the saddle restricted him to staying in that one place. In those days, many eq classes were judged on rail work only. But with the advent of more individual work in horsemanship classes, those saddles faded from popularity, especially with riders who use a saddle for more than one event, because there are times when a rider needs to become more ath-

letic and change position.

One thing that is a must is a suede seat, because that will help a rider adhere to the saddle far better than slick leather will. Stirrups should be hung so the rider can sit in balance with his legs under him.

You do not need a back cinch for horsemanship classes, but it's nice to have one because this cinch is useful in stabilizing the saddle in such classes as working cowhorse and reining.

Square skirts or round skirts are primarily a matter of preference, but round skirts usually work better than square

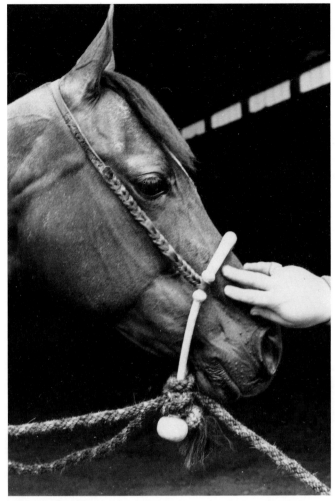

This is a hackamore, or jaquima. It should be adjusted so the bosal rests on the bridge of the nose, just above the cartilage. The bosal should also be pear-shaped, and it should fit loosely so the heel drops away when pressure is released.

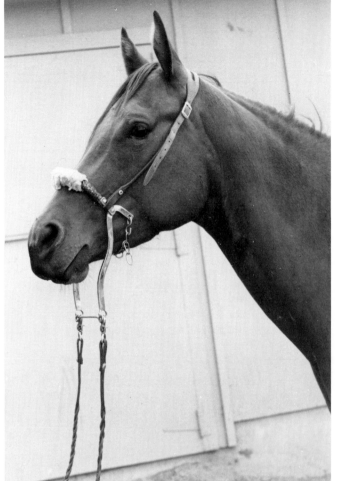

A hackamore bit adjusted correctly, with sheepskin on the nosepiece to prevent soring the nose. Called a brockamore years ago, the hackamore bit is frequently incorrectly referred to as a hackamore today. A hackamore bit always works on the leverage principle, while a hackamore does not.

Spade

Half-breed

Medium port

Low port

ones on short-backed horses like Arabians. By the same token, a square-skirt saddle looks better on a big Quarter Horse than does a saddle with little round skirts.

Silver, of course, is optional. I personally would rather see a well-made saddle with no silver than a saddle with cheap-looking silver, or with so much silver that it looks as if it's covered with pressed tin cans.

The design, such as roughout, flower

carving, basket stamping, etc., is also a matter of personal preference, but keep in mind that the better saddles have small but deeper tooling on pliable leather that is soft to the feel.

To sum up saddles: find the best-looking one you can afford, which fits both you and your horse, is comfortable, and allows you to ride correctly. In shopping, don't overlook the used saddle market. There are many fine used saddles for sale at reasonable prices. But, I

PARTS OF THE BIT

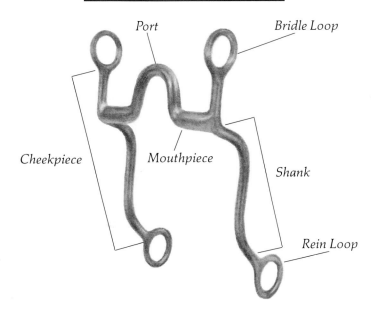

Port

Bridle Loop

Cheekpiece

Mouthpiece

Shank

Rein Loop

1/ A curb bit with a broken mouthpiece, popularly known as an Argentina snaffle. A similar style is known as the Tom Thumb snaffle.

never recommend buying any saddle without riding it first, preferably on your own horse to see if it fits him correctly. Many a saddle looks terrific sitting on a saddle rack or in the pages of a catalog, but can be uncomfortable to ride.

A good leather bridle is essential; nylon bridles don't cut it in judged events. Again, they should be neat and workmanlike, not gaudy, and should complement the horse. If he has a pretty little head, don't use a bridle that has thick, wide leather and huge buckles. Use one that's trim and neat. A horse with a big handsome head can wear a little bigger bridle. And if a horse's head leaves something to be desired in the looks department, a big bridle with big silver buckles can enhance his head.

Breast collars are not necessary, but can be a big help in keeping the saddle positioned correctly if the horse has mutton withers and the saddle tends to slip sideways. A breast collar is also a big

2/ A loose-jaw curb bit.

3/ A curb bit referred to as a grazing bit because of its swept-back shanks.

4/ A D-ring snaffle.

Bridles should be neat and workmanlike, and should complement the horse.

These two pictures show the correct (left) and incorrect positioning of the curb chain on a shank bit that has rein loops at the mouthpiece. Those loops are for reins, not the curb chain. Fastening the curb chain in the rein loops results in less leverage and, therefore, less control.

The correct position of a noseband for a tie-down, and the tie-down itself. The breast collar has a "keeper" for the tie-down. This handsome AQHA gelding is Double D Bambi Joe, owned by Tom and Betty Watt of Willow Springs Ranch in Colorado Springs.

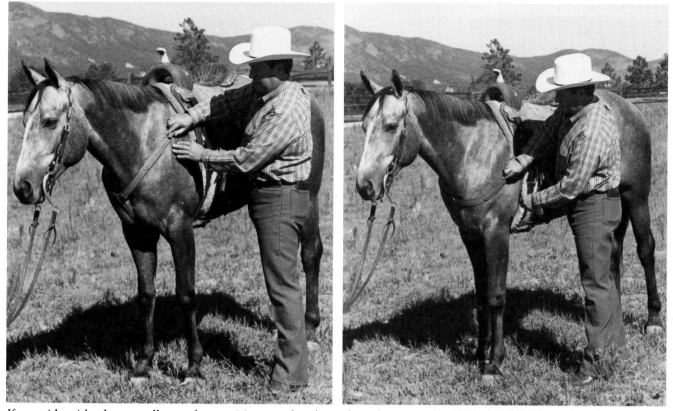

If you ride with a breast collar, make sure it's properly adjusted, as shown on the left. Dropping it so low (right) that it rides over the point of the shoulders can cause chafing, and detracts from the appearance of the horse.

help in mountain riding; it keeps the saddle from slipping back on steep, up-hill climbs.

If you use a breast collar in the show ring, it should be leather and similar in style to your saddle and bridle. Nylon breast collars with fleece lining, and mohair breast collars are not suitable in most judged events.

Whichever breast collar you use, stand back and see how it looks on the horse, because it can detract from his appearance. For example, if he has a low-set neck, a breast collar can magnify the problem. Or, if he has a long, pretty neck, it can make the neck look shorter.

If the rules require a rope or reata, carry the genuine item. Rope means a catch rope like cowboys use, not a

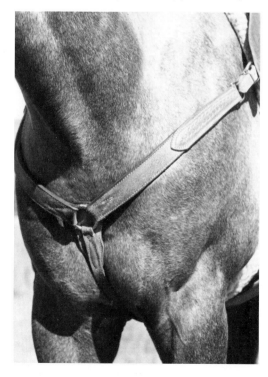

Some breast collars have a tie-down strap that attaches to the front cinch to keep the breast collar from riding too high and cutting off the horse's wind.

A lariat or catch rope neatly coiled.

A reata correctly coiled and tied on.

Not many judges will let you get away with using coiled-up baling twine when the rules call for a rope or reata.

coiled-up lead rope or piece of clothes-line. Learn how to coil a rope and reata properly, and how to tie them on correctly! Cowboys carry a rope so they can grab it and build a loop in a hurry before the critter escapes. This isn't possible if the rope is twisted, the honda is backwards, and it's hung upside down. If you want to impress the judge, coil and tie your rope or reata correctly.

Riders who compete in such classes as reining and cowhorse generally use bell boots and splint boots to protect the horse's front legs and feet, and skidboots on the back legs to protect his fetlocks when he stops hard.

As for saddle blankets and pads, styles come and go. Some of the popular pads in recent years have "gone" because they were irritating the backs of horses, even

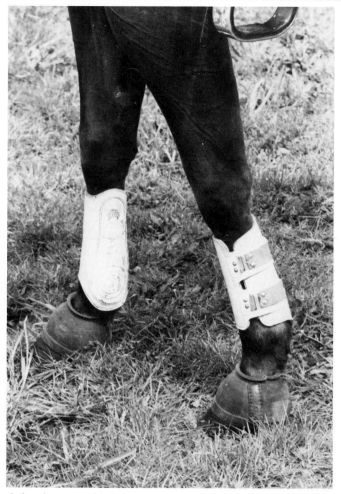

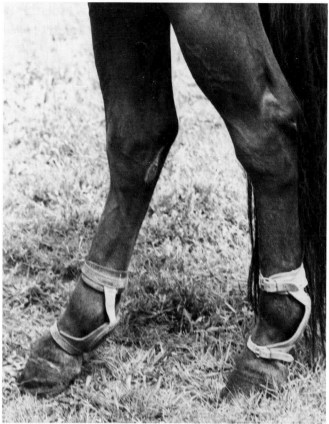

Skidboots protect the rear fetlocks from being burned in hard stops.

Splint boots and bell boots protect the front legs and pastern and coronet area.

though they looked classy. If in doubt as to what looks good, is comfortable to the horse, and will cause him no back problems, consider genuine Navajo saddle blankets. They are always in good taste. Also keep in mind that whether you need to use one or two blankets or pads will depend on your horse and how the saddle fits him.

Another point: keep your saddle and equipment clean. Cleanliness tells a judge if a rider cares about winning. If his gear is dirty or dusty, obviously he doesn't.

In summary, my best advice is to buy quality equipment that you would like your grandchildren to have and use.

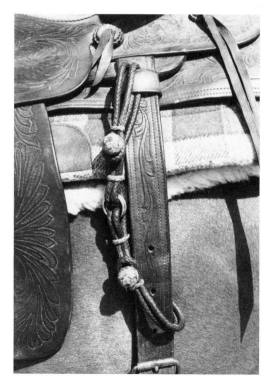

Here's a good way to carry hobbles when they are required.

5 SADDLING A HORSE

It takes longer to tell how to put the saddle on than to actually do it.

The simple act of saddling a horse becomes so routine that many experienced riders completely forget that this may seem complicated to the beginning rider. It takes longer to tell how to put the saddle on than to actually do it, but here are some step-by-step points to keep in mind to do a better job of saddling. Many of the old-timers will sheepishly admit they round off some corners, but they do know the right way. If you learn the right way, and then want to take some short cuts, it is up to you; but first you should consider these steps.

Make it automatic procedure to brush your horse before saddling. Get rid of any grime, caked dirt, or other rough spots that might cause saddle or cinch sores. Brush *with* the lay of the hair, and pay special attention to the horse's belly and cinch area. Also make it an automatic procedure to not only shake out the saddle blanket, but to look at the side of the blanket that goes next to the horse. Sandburs do not always shake out.

Then look at the lining of the saddle, especially if it has been on the ground. Burs or matted spots on the saddle lining can cause sores, too. After brushing,

1/ While Dad holds the mare, Jill Shrake brushes her off prior to saddling. Always brush the back and girth area extra carefully to remove dirt and mud that might cause sores.

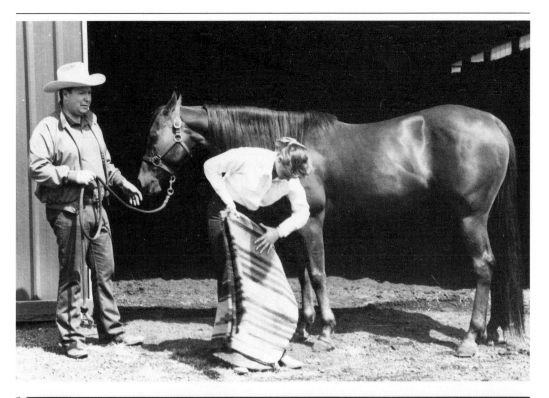

2/ Jill checks the saddle blankets to make sure they are free of burs and dirt.

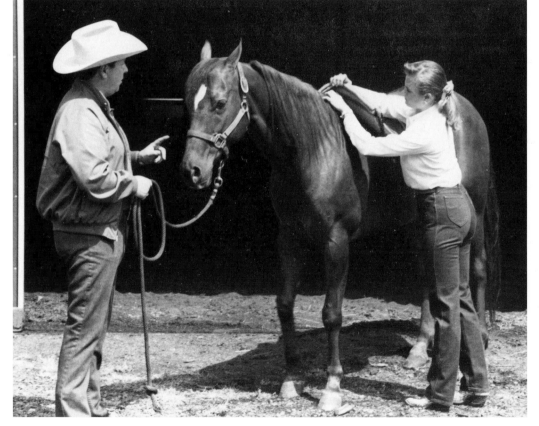

3/ Initially, Jill places the blankets a few inches too far forward, then slides them back into the correct position to flatten the hairs.

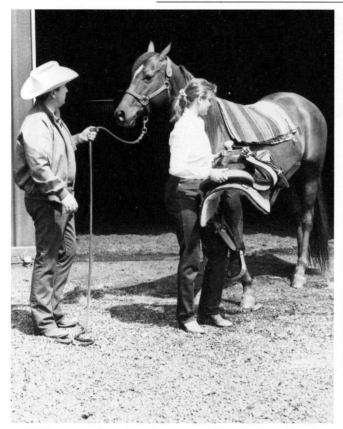

4/ With the cinch across the seat and the off stirrup hooked on the saddle horn . . .

5/ . . . Jill eases the saddle down on the back.

After brushing, shaking, and looking, you are ready to saddle up.

shaking, and looking, you are ready for the steps of actual saddling.

Place the saddle blanket up on the horse's back, several inches forward, then pull it towards the rear—*with* the lay of the horse's hair. If the design of your blanket is such that the center isn't marked, it is a good idea to mark the center so it will be balanced on the horse—not long on one side and short on the other.

Place the right stirrup and cinches over the seat of the saddle, and hold the saddle with your left hand in the gullet and your right hand on the rear skirts and housing. On saddles with a Cheyenne roll, you may want to grasp the cantle with the right hand. On new saddles, or saddles with short stirrups, it is better to loop the right stirrup over the saddle horn so it won't swing free and hit the horse as you put the saddle into place—which is one reason for holding the saddle by the gullet instead of holding it by the horn.

Then swing and *lift* the saddle into position easily—not suddenly, and not like you are trying to hit the horse with it. If you *lift* more than swing, and don't make it the first try, the saddle still doesn't bang into the horse and tend to make him nervous.

Throwing the saddle on, via the one-hand method, is not recommended for good horsemanship. You do see it done, and by some good riders, but it has too many drawbacks from the horsemanship standpoint. The saddle usually comes down with a bang on the horse's back, and he is usually hit with a stirrup, or cinch ring, or both, as they plop down on the off side of the horse.

With some practice, you can settle the saddle on the horse's back without plopping it down hard. You will develop the feel of lifting the saddle just the right height to clear the horse's withers.

Now comes the part most commonly omitted. Walk around to the off (right) side of your horse, pull the stirrup down, and the cinches, and see that nothing is twisted. Pull out any saddle strings that might be tucked under the saddle.

After this brief checkup, go back to the near (left) side of your horse. The saddle should be just slightly forward of where you want it, so grasp the horn and pommel and shake it back into position. With a well-used saddle, and a horse with good withers, you can feel the saddle slip into the correct spot—something like when your heel slips into place in a pair of tight boots.

Next, put a couple of fingers under the saddle blanket right over the horse's withers, and lift it up a bit. This lets air in under the blanket, and gives the withers some "working space."

Put your left stirrup up, over the horn or the saddle seat, and reach under the belly with the left hand for the cinch. The long latigo is in the right hand, and you then cinch the horse using whatever method you normally use.

Today, this is usually the tongued

6/ *Going to the off side, Jill unhooks the stirrup and drops the cinch so it hangs straight.*

7/ *Before cinching up, she uses her left hand to raise the saddle blanket over the withers to allow more clearance. This helps prevent chafing of the withers, and allows more air under the blanket to help keep the back comfortable.*

Two "old-timers" seldom seen anymore: a tackaberry and a cinch hook.

cinch ring, which works like a belt buckle. The latigo is looped through the cinch ring and the D ring of the saddle at least twice; when the cinch is snug enough, the tongue fits into the appropriate hole, and the end of the latigo is looped through the keeper on the saddle. Once the tongue is in the hole, be sure and tighten the latigo down over the tongue, so the tongue can't slip out. That could result in the cinch working loose—and a wreck.

Seldom seen anymore are the tackaberry and cinch hook. They were devices designed to save the rider the trouble of running the latigo through the cinch ring two or three times every time he saddled. The curved hook (see drawings) catches and holds the cinch ring, and the latigo is then either buckled or tied—but it remains looped in the cinch hook or tackaberry.

Something always handy to know is the latigo tie, which is shown in an accompanying illustration. Even if your cinch ring has a tongue, sometimes it's safest to also tie off the latigo.

Regardless of how you secure the cinch, remember to cinch up in at least two or three stages. Some horses are what's called "cinchy." Immediately cinching them up tight can result in their having some type of bad reaction, like rearing, or dropping to their knees. So cinch up those horses easily; tighten the cinch just enough so the saddle won't slip, walk the horse about a dozen steps; then tighten the cinch again.

Now fasten the rear cinch if your saddle has a double rigging. Draw it up so it is just snug against the belly, but not tight. You will see some riders who let the rear cinch hang up to eight inches below the belly. This is dangerous. If a horse should kick at a fly, or slip or fall in rough country, he can easily get a back foot through the rear cinch. It can also happen when you are crossing water and then you're in for a rodeo, with injuries very likely to you and your horse.

There should always be a connecting strap between the front and back

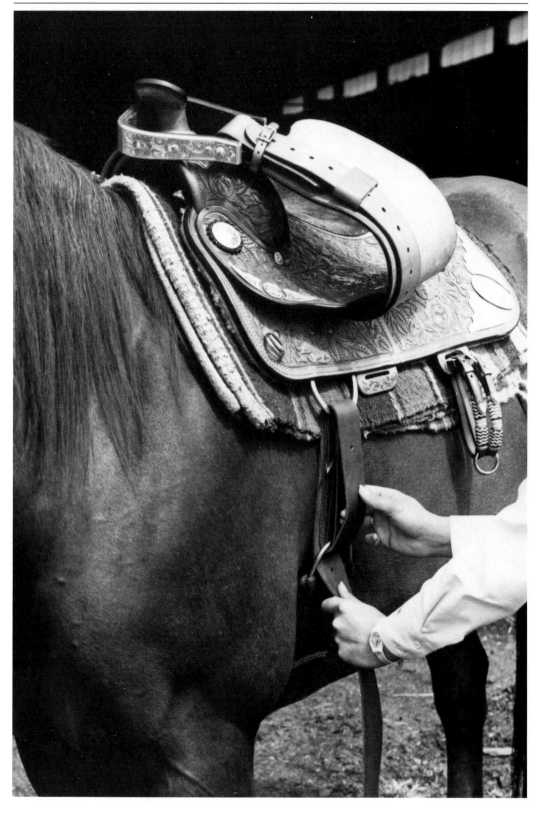

8/ Jill takes two wraps of the latigo through the cinch ring and tightens the cinch.

Some horses are what's called cinchy.

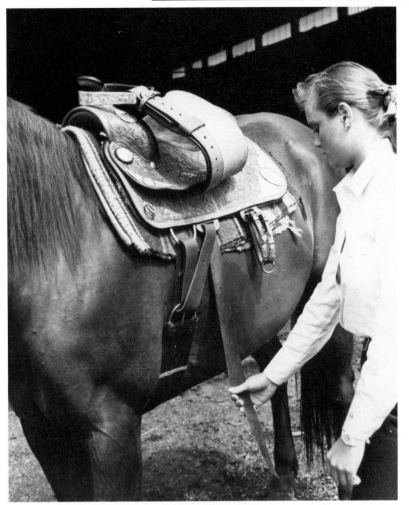

9/ After fitting the tongue into the appropriate hole in the latigo and snugging it down, Jill runs the extra latigo through the keeper. The keeper on this saddle is located on the skirt to keep the extra latigo out of sight for an overall neater appearance.

Here's how you tie off the latigo if you don't use a cinch with a tongue. Take the latigo through the D ring and to the left, bring it around to the right, go through the D ring from the inside, drop the latigo through the loop you have formed, and snug it down tight.

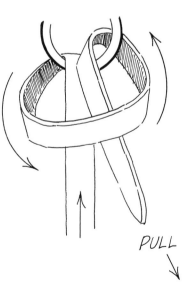

PULL

cinches, so the latter can't slip too far back. This strap should also be flat against the belly so brush or limbs can't get snagged in it.

If you are riding with a breast collar, that's the last thing you fasten. Many riders like to use a breast collar because it helps to keep the saddle in position, especially when riding in hilly or mountain country. One thing to watch: do not let the breast collar ride up so high it pushes against the horse's windpipe. To prevent this, many breast collars have a tie-down strap that runs between the front legs and snaps to the front cinch. This strap should be snug, but not so tight it chafes the horse.

The horse is saddled now, but there's one more step: untrack him by leading him a few steps. Frequently you can take up another notch in the cinch after walking him a few steps. If not, check the cinch anyway, then check again after riding a short distance. Many horses take in air and sort of hold their breath while being cinched; then they exhale, and the cinch is too loose.

Compared to saddling, unsaddling is a snap, but there are three important points to always remember:

1/ If your saddle has a back cinch, always unbuckle it first. Next, unbuckle the breast collar. Last, undo the front cinch. Why? Suppose you have loosened the front cinch and something startles the horse and he jumps. The saddle can slip, but it can't fall free because it's still secured to the horse by the back cinch. Here's usually what happens: it slides under the horse's belly, scares him, he

Secure the breast collar after cinching up.

bolts and runs, and it's good-by saddle. Hopefully the horse won't get hurt, too.

This is the same reason why, when saddling, you always secure the front cinch first—then the back cinch. And when you stop on the trail to rest awhile and loosen the front cinch, the back cinch should be completely unbuckled.

2/ If you ride with a breast collar, unfasten it before you un-cinch—so if the saddle starts to slide while you are un-cinching, it will fall free of the horse.

3/ When taking the saddle off, lift it above the horse's withers, and then off his back. Do not drag it over the withers as that can irritate the horse. Lifting the saddle over the withers is good horse-manship!

If you ride with a back cinch, ALWAYS fasten it after securing the front cinch. And when you unsaddle, ALWAYS unbuckle the back cinch first. The back cinch should be snug against the belly, as should the connecting strap between the front and back cinches.

6

BRIDLING A HORSE

Some horses are difficult to bridle because they do not like having their ears handled.

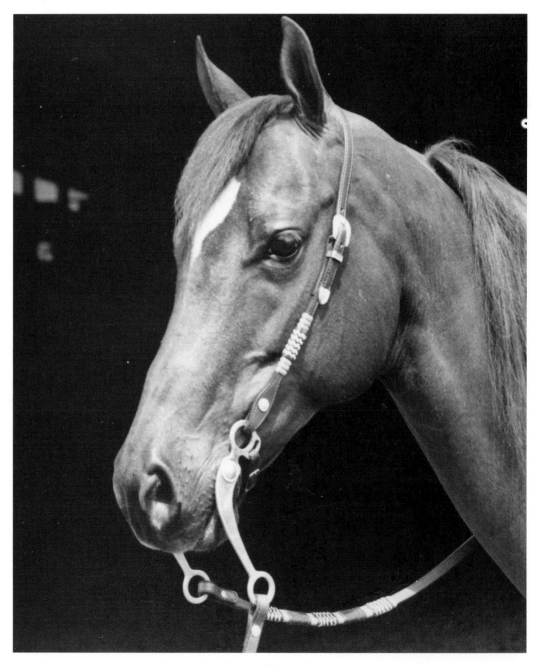

A neat, workmanlike bridle with silver buckles.

There are two popular types of bridles used by western horsemen: the browband-type and the split-ear type. Which to use is primarily a matter of personal preference, but some horsemen prefer a browband bridle because they feel it allows the bit to hang more evenly in the mouth. However, the careful horseman makes sure the bit hangs straight when a split-ear bridle is used.

The browband bridle comes equipped with a throatlatch, as do some split-ear bridles. The throatlatch prevents the horse from rubbing the bridle off too easily, but since a horse should really never be tied with a bridle on, this is of little importance. On the other hand, a throatlatch will help keep the bridle on if, while being ridden, the horse puts his head down to rub it on a front leg, or if the cheekpiece is snagged by a limb or branch in rough country.

The photos show the accepted method for bridling the average horse. Although many good horsemen simply drop the halter when they bridle the horse, it's a good practice to always buckle the halter around horse's neck so he can't get away. This is especially true if you are in the open, and not in an enclosed area. If something should startle the horse at that very moment when he has neither halter nor bridle on, you could be in for a long chase.

Some horses are difficult to bridle because they do not like having their ears handled. Often this results from a careless person mangling the ears while bridling the horse. If this practice continues, the horse reflects his discomfort by making it very difficult to get the bridle on.

This problem can be tough to correct. Some horse owners have solved the problem by getting such a horse accustomed to having his ears stroked gently, without trying to bridle him. Doing this while standing on a bucket or sitting astride another horse will make it easier since the horse will undoubtedly try to put his ears out of reach.

This project can take time to accomplish. To ride the horse in the meantime, use a bridle that has no browband or earpiece. Unbuckle the cheekpiece, slip the bit into the mouth, bring the crownpiece behind the ears, and rebuckle. This way, you don't have to touch the ears.

1/ Jill Shrake unbuckles the halter and . . .

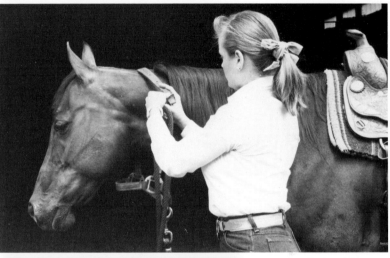

2/ . . . Rebuckles it around the neck for safety's sake while she bridles this mare.

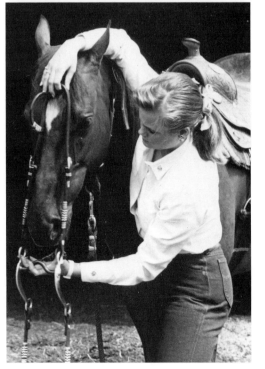

3/ Hold the crownpiece with your right hand while your left hand separates the bit from the curb chain.

37

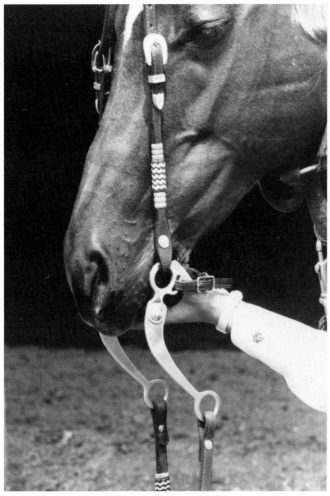

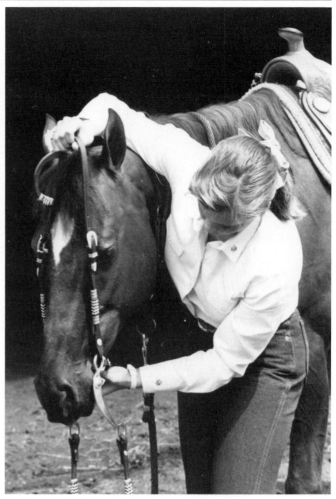

4/ Many horses will automatically open their mouths when they feel the bit against their teeth. But when a horse doesn't, use your thumb in the corner of the mouth (where there are no teeth) to make him open his mouth.

5/ As the bit slides in, pull the crownpiece up.

6/ Carefully slide the crownpiece over the left ear.

If a horse just plain doesn't want to be bridled, there's another method you can try. This one requires leaving the halter on the horse and running the lead rope down between the front legs and up to the saddle horn where it is dallied or tied in a quick-release knot. The rope should be tied with enough slack so the horse can raise his head a few inches, but no farther. If he's tied so short he can't move his head at all, he might panic. In fact, it's a good idea to tie the horse this way, then let him move around in a corral to find out his head is tied down, before you try to bridle him.

Since he can't get his head up, he will be a lot easier to get the bridle on. Then, untie the lead rope, leave the halter on, and you're ready to ride. When the average horse finds out he cannot fight being bridled, he generally will stand quietly after a few sessions of having his head tied down.

7/ Then hold the crownpiece in your left hand while the right reaches for the other ear.

8/ Gently fit the right ear into the earpiece.

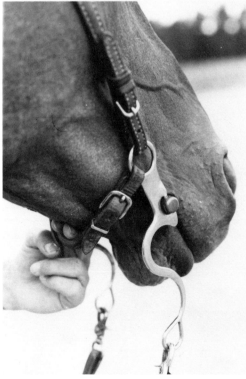

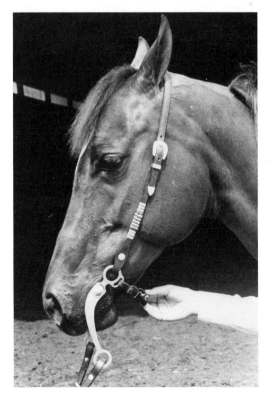

You should be able to fit two fingers between the curb chain and the chin. This one is too loose. Note that this bit has separate slots for fastening the curb chain; this prevents the corners of the mouth from being pinched.

This curb strap is adjusted correctly.

7 MOUNTING AND DISMOUNTING

From this position you can watch both ends of the horse.

For years, the correct method for mounting required the rider to stand facing the rear of the horse, so the rider could clearly watch the hindquarters and dodge any kicks coming his way. But this method created two problems: 1/ The rider could not see the front end, which can bite, and 2/ As the rider mounted and his foot turned toward the front of the horse, the toe of his boot invariably poked the horse in the ribs. This usually caused him to move, a no-no whether you are mounting under the watchful eyes of a judge, or heading out on a pleasure ride.

Today, correct mounting calls for the rider to stand facing the horse. From this position, you can watch both ends of the horse. Your left hand should hold the reins. The reins should not be so tight they pull the horse back, nor so loose you cannot immediately check the horse

if he starts to move off. The right hand grasps the saddle horn.

The left foot goes into the stirrup directed toward the cinch so the toe will not bump the horse in the belly. Now step up quickly and efficiently, using your right leg for most of your boosting power. Do *not* pull yourself up. Keep your shoulders square, your eyes straight ahead, and make sure your right leg clears the horse's rump as you swing it over. As you settle into the saddle, your right foot immediately picks up the stirrup.

If you are riding with split reins, you are in position and ready to go, unless you need to adjust the length of the reins a little. If you are riding with reins and romal, pick up the romal with your right hand and move it over to the off side of the horse. Remember: Most rules specify that there should be about 16 inches of

1/ This is the first in a sequence of photos with Todd Bergen, who shows the proper dismount and mount with romal reins. The first step is bringing the romal to the left side.

2/ Take up reins until left hand has firm contact with horse's mouth. Left hand remains on the horse's neck.

3/ Right hand goes on horn and right leg swings over. Shoulders remain even as rider continues looking forward.

4/ Step down, continuing to face same direction as horse.

5/ Loop reins over the horn.

6/ Walk forward while running right hand down the left rein and address judge. Never turn loose of the reins.

slack in the romal—between your left hand and your right hand.

To dismount, reverse the procedure. Move the romal over to the left side, put your right hand on the horn, and step down. Loop the reins over the horn, step forward while sliding your right hand down the left rein, and address the judge.

If you have split reins, step down while continuing to hold both reins in your left hand. When you step forward to address the judge, you can leave the right rein looped over the saddle horn while you continue to hold the left rein. However, some judges like to see you remove both reins and hold them. When you do this, you should "mark" the right rein; then when you remount, you know exactly where to grasp that rein with

7/ To remount, turn into the horse and put your left hand on the rein as your right hand comes off, and run your left hand up the rein.

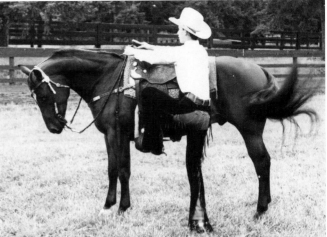

8/ *Unloop reins off the horn and hold in your left hand.*

9/ *Facing the horse, maintain light contact with mouth with left hand on the reins, and put right hand on the horn. Step into stirrup, with your toe directed toward the cinch.*

10/ *Step up, and be sure to keep right leg above the horse's croup, and settle lightly into saddle.*

11/ *Bring romal over to right side.*

your left hand so it is the correct length. This adds a touch of finesse to your horsemanship. The accompanying pictures show how to do it.

In some shows, especially 4-H shows, it is standard practice to check the curb chain, to make sure it is still secure, and the cinch, to make sure it is still tight, before you remount. But in many of the larger open shows, this isn't required. Your best bet: Check to see what is expected before you ride into the arena in a horsemanship class.

If you have trouble mounting easily and correctly, practice it repeatedly. For students with this problem, I sometimes have them practice until they can mount and dismount *without* a cinch on the saddle!

What about a horse that won't stand

1/ When dismounting with split reins, put your left hand on the neck and right hand on horn. Maintain light contact with horse's mouth.

2/ Swing your right leg over and keep your shoulders square. The right leg should not be straight because that would cause the shoulders to drop, and would make dismounting stiff instead of fluid and natural.

for mounting? He is a problem, and will cost you points in a horsemanship class. Some horses are so bad they are dangerous. In many cases, this problem is inadvertently caused by the rider who lets the horse start moving as soon as he's in the saddle. Pretty soon the horse doesn't wait for the rider to get in the saddle before he moves. And it can get progressively worse until the horse moves off as soon as the rider puts his foot in the stirrup.

Although this isn't a training book, there are a couple of things that can be tried with a horse like this.

No. 1: Put the horse in a small pen, like 15 x 15 feet, or a stall so he can't go anywhere, and mount and dismount several dozen times every day. When the horse even *thinks* about moving, check him immediately, even if you are only halfway up. Since the horse can't go anywhere, he's more apt to remain standing still. Then dismount and re-

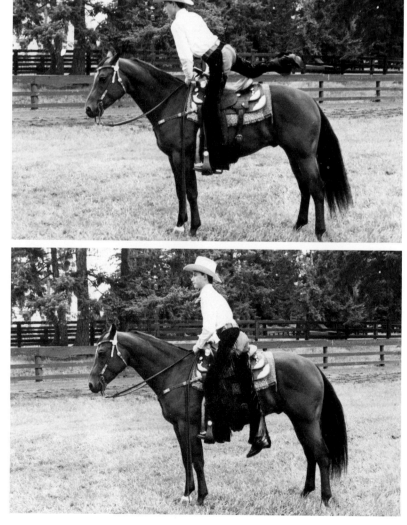

3/ Step down with your body facing forward.

4/ At this point, you can leave the right rein over the saddle horn and step forward holding the left rein, or take them both down as Todd will do.

5/ Todd moves the reins forward in his left hand, and then momentarily holds the right rein in his right hand . . . .

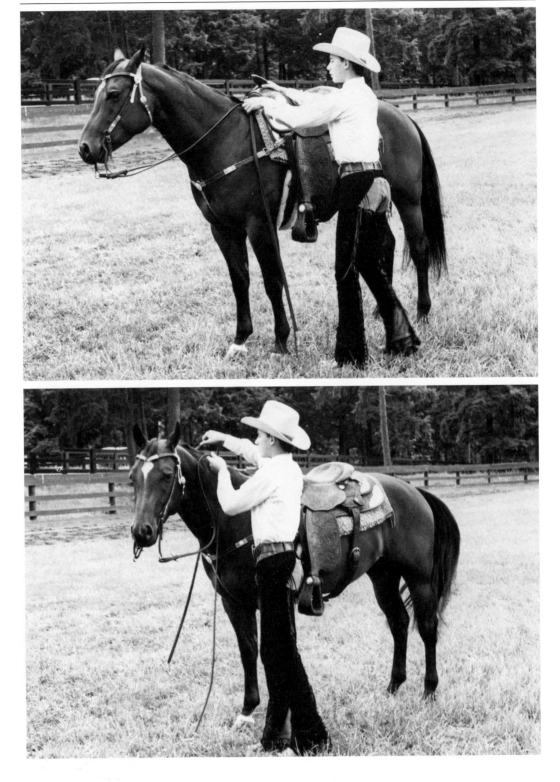

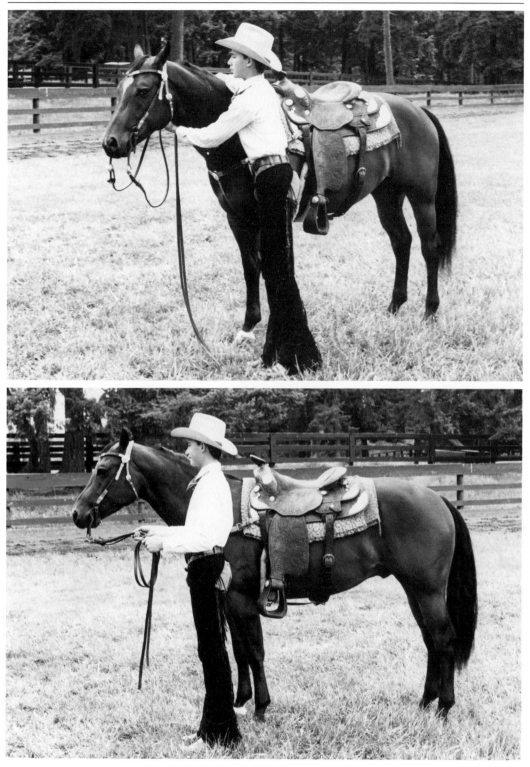

6/ . . . As the left hand reaches under the neck for the right rein at the exact spot where the right hand held it. This is called "marking." Its advantage: When the rider turns to remount, he knows exactly where to pick up and hold the right rein for proper adjustment of length.

7/ Todd addresses the judge, holding the reins just behind the bit with his right hand, and the ends of his reins in the left hand. Mounting with split reins is just the reverse of dismounting.

The old style of mounting called for the rider to face the rear and swing into the saddle. In today's horsemanship classes, this is incorrect.

peat. When he stands quietly, move to a larger pen and repeat the lessons until he stands like a statue.

No. 2: Try variations of No. 1 by tying the horse to a post and mounting and dismounting dozens of times; or, get him hobble-broke, and then mount and dismount repeatedly while he is hobbled. Since he can't move while tied or hobbled, it should become ingrained in his brain that he stands still while you mount.

Once he will stand without being tied, hobbled, or positioned in a small pen, untie him, or remove the hobbles, and

When the rider's toe is directed toward the cinch when he mounts, he will avoid jabbing the horse and causing him to move.

Dragging yourself into the saddle is a sloppy way to mount. In addition, with your left hand on the saddle, you can't stop the horse if he moves off.

see how he does. If he won't cooperate, repeat the lessons, or seek professional help from a trainer.

Once he will stand quietly, ALWAYS make him stand still for a couple of minutes after you are in the saddle. Teach him that he doesn't move until you say so. Also be careful not to cause him to move by checking the reins too tightly, or pulling him sideways by struggling to get into the saddle.

It goes without saying that one usually mounts from the left side of the horse. However, any well-broke horse should stand still for mounting from either side. And there are occasions when riding in hills or mountains that one should mount from the right side, if that is the uphill side of the horse. If he happens to be standing on ground higher than you are, don't struggle to climb up into the saddle on the left side. Just walk around to the uphill side and step on easily.

When trail riding, the correct side for mounting is the uphill side.

8 BASIC POSITION: FEET & LEGS

This photo shows excellent foot and leg position.

Just as you build a house from the foundation up, you build proper position in the saddle starting with your feet. When the feet are positioned incorrectly, it is darn near impossible to correctly position the lower legs, knees, upper legs, seat, body, and hands. And if your feet are wobbly—moving back and forth—it will be impossible to keep your legs and body secure, resulting in unsteady hands.

Thus your feet, which might seem of little importance in terms of correct horsemanship, actually play a major role in how well you ride.

Correct foot position starts with proper length of stirrup. For years, one rule-of-thumb has stated that the bottom of the stirrup should hit at or just below your ankle bone. While this is generally true, it is not always accurate . . . especially on broad-backed horses, or those with big round barrels.

The guideline I follow is this: when the stirrups are adjusted correctly, the angle of the upper leg (from hip to knee) should be almost the same as that of the lower leg (from knee to ankle). If you have this angle, and if you can stand in your stirrups with your heels down and slip your hand underneath your seat, your stirrup length is correct.

This length puts your feet under you, not ahead of you or behind you. When the feet, legs, and body are positioned correctly, an imaginary vertical line can be dropped from the ear down through the shoulder, upper arm, hip, and heel.

When the feet, legs, and body are positioned correctly, an imaginary line can be dropped from the ear down through the shoulder, upper arm, hip, and heel. The broomstick illustrates the line from the hip to the heel.

You sometimes hear that the lower legs should hang straight down from the knees, but this isn't correct for equitation because it usually puts the feet ahead of the seat. This makes you more of a passenger rather than a rider moving as one with the horse. If your feet are behind your seat, this causes you to tilt forward. As a test, stand in your stirrups. If you find yourself leaning or falling back, your feet are too far in front of you. If you lean or fall forward, your feet are behind you. Organize your legs so you can stand straight up with ease, then sit down in the saddle, maintaining that leg position.

You sometimes see riders using a stirrup length shorter than normal. This is true with ropers who stand in their stirrups while swinging a loop, and with cutting horse riders. The shorter your stirrups, the more secure your seat will be. If you're on a cutting horse that's diving back and forth, a shorter stirrup will give you a lot more security. The same is true when working cattle in a cowhorse class, or when running barrels.

A reining horse rider might also use a little shorter stirrup because there are times, such as when stopping, that he wants to get his feet out in front of him

An exaggerated example of a leg too far forward.

and brace himself a little bit against the cantle. There are also times when he wants to ride behind the horse's center of gravity in order to drive the horse forward (with his legs) and lift the front end a little.

For horsemanship classes, riders should use a standard stirrup with about a 2½-inch or 3-inch tread. Oxbow stirrups are not satisfactory because feet are rammed "home" in these stirrups . . . meaning all the way to the boot heels. This is not correct for equitation; besides, a rider loses some of the elasticity and feel in the calves of his legs when his feet are rammed home.

The balls of the feet should be on the tread of the stirrups. While the feet should be parallel to the horse, the toes can be turned slightly out to facilitate

Here's a leg that's too far back. I have noticed that some stock seat riders who also ride saddle seat seem to pick up the bad habit of having their feet too far back.

correct positioning of the lower legs, knees, and upper legs. But if the toes are pointed too far out, your knees and thighs will be rolled too far out while the calves of your lower legs are rolled too far in. If your toes turn in, this causes the calves of your legs to roll out.

The calves should always have light contact with the sides of the horse . . . I like to refer to this as having a "wrap" on the horse. But by contact, I don't mean pressure. It's like gently touching your arm with the opposite hand; there's no pressure, just a light feel. It should be the same with the calves of your legs on the sides of the horse. Then your legs are in position to immediately apply pressure when necessary, with no movement perceptible to the judge—part of the invisible aids so necessary to win horseman-

Todd Bergen shows one test to determine if your stirrups are the correct length. If they are, you should be able to stand and slide your entire hand comfortably between you and the saddle.

ship classes today.

To make it easier to keep the feet positioned correctly, the stirrups should hang at a right angle to the horse. Unfortunately, the stirrups on most western saddles do not hang this way naturally. Trying to keep your feet positioned correctly when the stirrups are forcing them the wrong way is difficult for even an accomplished rider. Yet you see this happening in class after class.

To make the stirrups hang correctly, the stirrup leathers need to be soaked in water (just insert them into a bucket for a few minutes), twisted into the correct position, and held in that position with a broomstick while they dry. Depending on the saddle, the stirrup leathers might need this treatment every few months. When a saddle will not be used for a while, it should be stored with a broomstick run through the stirrups to keep them hanging straight.

Once the feet are positioned correctly, the heels should be dropped so they are

The balls of the feet should be on the tread of the stirrups, and the heels should always be lower than the toes.

52

Riding with the toes too far out also rolls the knees too far out. I'm sliding my hand under Todd's knee to show how much space there is between the saddle and his knee.

The calves of the legs should always have light contact with the horse. This is not possible when the lower legs are too far out, with the toes pointed in.

lower than the toes. Keeping the heels down stretches the muscles in your lower legs so you can use them more effectively, helps to steady both your feet and legs, and helps keep your knees locked in.

Although knees should be flat against the saddle, they should be relaxed. You sometimes hear beginning riders being told, "Grip with your knees!" This isn't good advice. Gripping with the knees results in tense leg muscles, especially in the thighs, and tense muscles quickly tire. Besides, one stays on a horse through balance and correct position, not by gripping.

In this respect, riding a horse can be compared to riding a bicycle. You don't stay on a bike by putting a death grip on the handlebars and squeezing the frame with your legs. Balance and coordination keep you upright.

If your feet, calves, and knees are positioned correctly, your thighs will be automatically positioned correctly—which means they will be rolled snugly against the saddle. But here again, they should be relaxed, not tense.

This is the leg position I like to see for maintaining light contact with the calves.

Gripping with the knees results in tense leg muscles.

To make stirrups hang correctly, soak the stirrup leathers and even the lower part of the fenders in a bucket of water. Then twist the stirrups into the correct position and slide a broomstick through them.

To initially achieve correct positioning of the feet and legs requires concentration—and work. It doesn't come easily. There are also exercises you can do, which we will cover in a later chapter. At first, you will have sore muscles, but this work will pay dividends in the long run when your feet and legs automatically assume the correct position, and maintain it. It will become second nature.

While striving for correct position, also work to keep your legs and feet quiet. If your feet—your foundation—continually move back and forth as the horse moves, you cannot achieve a secure seat in the saddle.

A small rider on a big-barreled horse can have a difficult time maintaining the correct leg wrap, but Melissa Coffey shows a good wrap.

9 BASIC POSITION: ARMS & HANDS

There are times when it makes good sense to use two hands.

When riding with split reins, the accepted position for the free hand in a horsemanship class is slightly above the thigh.

For most judged events in the show ring, rules stipulate that only one hand can be used on the reins. But there are exceptions. In classes which permit use of a snaffle or hackamore, two hands can be used; in fact, two hands should always be used when riding with this type of headgear.

Two hands can also be used in timed events, such as barrel racing, and in everyday riding. Since western horses are usually neck-reined, many beginning

riders feel that it is taboo to use two hands on the reins. This is not true, and there are times when it makes good sense to use two hands. For example, if you're trying to get Ol' Bay turned around and he isn't responding to the neck-rein, use both hands and pull his head around with a direct rein. Or if you're riding an iron-jawed horse you can't get stopped, use both hands.

For purposes of this book, we'll assume you are riding in a judged event,

This is the correct manner in which to hold split reins (left) and reins and romal.

and can use only one hand on the reins. Both of your upper arms should hang in a relaxed manner right next to your body. From the side, the judge wants to see only one line from the waist up; if an elbow is in front of or behind your body, he sees two lines.

Do not clamp your arms tight against your body; this makes you look stiff. On the other hand, don't relax them so much they flap in the air when the horse trots or lopes. The elbows of some riders flap so hard, they look like a duck taking off from a pond.

The position of your rein hand can vary slightly, according to whether you are riding with split reins or with reins and a romal (ro-MAUL). The hand of the romal rider is right over the horn, just high enough to clear it. The hand of the split-rein rider is just in front of the horn.

Why the difference? The rein hand should be low—as the old adage says, "A low hand means a low head." And a split-rein rider can keep his hand low.

With reins and romal, however, the reins come up through the hand, which is held upright. Therefore the hand must be a little higher in order for the reins to clear the saddle horn.

Many riders prefer a romal for several reasons. For example, the romal allows the length of the reins to be easily adjusted. This isn't so important in a rail class where you only walk, trot, and lope; but in classes where you must execute circles, changes, stops, and turnarounds, it is a definite advantage.

The romal hand can rest on the thigh, or be held just above it.

When split reins are held in the left hand, the ends of the reins should fall on the left side. And when the horse is moving, the rein hand should not be any higher than shown here.

Riding with reins and romal also gives both hands something to do; this tends to give a rider more balance and square-ness, and helps keep both shoulders in line. A split-rein rider has a tendency to "lead" with the shoulder of his rein hand.

The non-rein hand of the romal rider holds the romal, and rests on the rider's thigh. Most rule books stipulate that there should be at least 16 inches of slack between the rider's two hands.

In years past, split-rein riders had a terrible time deciding how to carry the free hand. Some held it across their chest, as if the arm were broken and in a cast. This gives the rider the appearance of being stiff and unnatural.

Today, the accepted position is to drop the free hand so it rests naturally on the thigh, then raise it slightly, as shown in the photo on page 56.

Whether you ride with split reins or a romal, keep your rein hand relaxed. Do not clench the reins tightly, because this will tense your arm and upper body, and your every signal to the horse, through the bit, will be hard instead of soft.

When rules stipulate that only one hand can be used on the reins, it is op-tional as to which hand. It has always been traditional to use the left hand be-cause most people are right-handed; this leaves the right hand free for such jobs as roping or opening a gate. But it is per-missible to use your right hand if you are left-handed, or simply feel more com-fortable with your right hand on the reins.

When riding with split reins, you are allowed to use one finger between the reins. This can be an advantage when you are on a horse that does not neck-rein well. By manipulating the reins, you can use somewhat of a direct-rein as well as a neck-rein.

When you are using split reins, are holding them in your left hand, and are using one finger between them, the ends of the reins fall on the left side. If you hold the reins in your right hand, the

Your upper arms should hang in a relaxed manner next to your body.

Always check the rules under which your class will be judged.

ends hang on the right side . . . and if a rope or reata is attached to your saddle, then it must be on the left side, not the right.

The preceding is true in both the AHSA and AQHA. However, AHSA allows riders the option of using split reins as they would a romal. In other words, you can hold the reins in either hand, with the hand *around* the reins (no finger between them), and the ends of the reins in the other hand, just as you would a romal. At present, AQHA does not allow this option.

This is a good reason why you should check the rules under which your equitation or horsemanship class will be judged. Rules vary between associations, and are sometimes changed when associations update their rule books.

10 USE OF THE HANDS

It is the hands that determine how smoothly and softly the horse responds.

The hands are the primary means of communication between the rider and horse. Even though the feet, legs, and body weight also play a role, it is the hands that primarily tell the horse what the rider is asking, and it is the hands that determine how smoothly and softly the horse responds. This is where the real feel of riding begins.

Many people, however, do not understand what good hands are. They believe that good hands are those that never touch the bit, and so they ride and show with a lot of slack in their reins.

I think the best explanation is this: Good hands are those that communicate and relay messages from the rider to the horse with a consistent and secure feel. This means you should always have a little feel of the outer corners of the mouth . . . just a very light touch. You can even have a small amount of slack in the reins and still maintain this feel. To understand what I mean, put your hand lightly on the arm of your chair while reading this. You have light contact, but

Horsemanship judges like to see the rein hand held right over the horn, and at the same angle as the lower arm. In other words, there should be a straight line from the elbow to the hand. Do not bend the wrist.
Photo by Steve White

you are not pulling.

Then when you ask the horse to slow or stop, or when you gather him up to ask for the lope, you need only to barely move your hand. It is a movement imperceptible to the judge.

If your horse has a light, responsive mouth, your messages to him through the reins should only be as firm as necessary. That is, you only apply the amount of pressure through your hands that you need. For example, if you need only three pounds of pressure to ask the horse to stop, you don't apply thirty pounds.

I like to use the analogy of pulling a carrot out of the ground. If you grab hold of the top and jerk, the top will come off. But if you take a firm hold and pull gently, the entire carrot will slide out of the ground.

The horse reacts the same way. Grab hold of the bit with a ten-pound jerk and the horse's head will come up, he will get stiff through the jaw, poll, and neck, and his back will hollow out.

On the other hand, if you are only applying three pounds of pressure and the horse is running off, you've got to be firmer and apply more pressure. So you apply whatever amount of pressure is necessary to get the job done. But, the ideal is a continual light feel of the corners of the mouth, with the horse responding to whatever you ask with no

If your horse has a light, responsive mouth, you can get spectacular results with a very light pull—as Tim McQuay is doing here. Tim, from Maple Plain, Minn., is riding Zan Buck Too, owned at the time by Eric and Brian Palen of Cheyenne, Wyoming. **Photo by Harold Campton**

61

The rein hand should remain as steady as possible because it gives the horse balance and security.

tail—between the bridle reins and bit, and then see who could slide their horses the farthest, or spin the fastest, without breaking the hair.

But you can't do this if you ride with a lot of slack in your reins. That's sort of like a waterskier waiting on the beach with ten feet of slack in the pull rope. If the boat roars off and eats up that slack, the waterskier is jerked off his feet instead of gliding gradually into the water.

Romal reins give a horse and rider a little more balance and finesse, and that's one reason why a lot of top horsemanship riders use them. The rein hand absolutely never has to move, because the hand holding the romal does the adjusting. It's easy to take up the slack, and when you want to give the horse a little more slack, all you need to do is loosen the hand holding the romal, and the weight of the reins drops them through the rein hand.

However, those who are skilled with split reins can use them beautifully. Because you are allowed to keep one finger between split reins, it's easier to shorten one rein when necessary . . . such as shortening the right rein to circle to the right, to keep the horse's head a little to the inside of the circle.

Of course, the ultimate goal is for your hands not to appear to move at all. Perfection in the show ring is the invisible aid. If your horse can circle, change leads, spin, roll-back, and stop—all without your rein hand seeming to move, you will be tough to beat. But keep in mind that you can only do this on a finished, well-trained horse. When riding a green colt, or an older horse with a problem, you often have to use both hands, and use them well out of the accepted normal position.

One thing I want to explain is my term "slow the hand down." Many a rider has hands too quick; they might not jerk or snatch the reins, but will still move too fast, and out of rhythm with the horse. To teach a rider to slow his hand down, I'll have him walk and count cadence with the horse: 1, 2, 3, 4, and 1, 2, 3, 4, and . . . . I will have him shorten his reins in cadence with the horse's walk.

At the trot, which is a two-beat gait, the rider must learn to do it faster, but still in rhythm with the horse. Assume the horse is jogging and the rider wants

visible movement of your rein hand.

You don't get into the horse's inner mouth until you need to push him into the bridle more for increased collection, a lead change, or long stop when more contact helps balance the horse.

The rein hand should remain as steady as possible because that gives the horse security. This means the hand should basically stay in the same place, and not be four inches above the saddle horn for one cue and two inches below the horn the next time. Having security from a steady hand will help the horse relax in his jaw, poll, and neck.

How you hold the reins plays a role, too. A romal rein, for example, should not be held strictly in the palm of the hand in a vise-like grip. Instead, it should be held in the fingers, which are more sensitive than the palm, or fist. Your fingers should just flutter a little bit to communicate with the horse. To communicate through your wrist, you have to move your entire arm, which moves your shoulder.

The beauty of a well-trained West Coast romal-style horse is that he responds to just a flutter of the fingers. In fact, the old Spanish vaqueros used to tie a strand of horsehair—from the mane or

Here's a good example of how to hold split reins. Many riders like to use these reins because rules permit use of one finger between them.

This rider is maintaining light contact with the horse's mouth, and her hand is square and steady, yet not rigid; it is yielding to the horse's mouth. Overall, this rider shows very good positioning, but her eyes should be looking straight ahead.

to shorten his reins. There's a split-second when both diagonal feet are off the ground at the same time, and that's when the rider should take up on the reins. This way, it's a natural gathering of the horse in rhythm with how he's moving—instead of doing it against the motion of the horse.

At the lope, gather the reins when the horse gathers himself and comes off the ground.

The more you can take up or loosen the reins with the rhythm of the horse, the more cadence the horse will have and the steadier he will go. Once he is steady and moving with the rider, then he will be relaxed and supple.

To get a better idea of what I mean, try this. Assume you are trotting and want to stop. Sit down in the saddle, and apply light pressure with your rein hand while saying *whooooaaaaa*. When your voice is soft and slow, like this, your hand will be soft and slow.

Now go try it again, and this time, command *WHOA!* You'll find that your hand grabbed hold quick, just like your voice, and the horse probably popped his head and stiffened his entire body.

If your hand is slow, and if the pull from your hand comes from the same position every time, and has a quietness to it, the horse will develop confidence

in you, will bridle up nicely, round his back, and work softly and fluidly.

A lot of people say that those with good hands are born that way, but I think that's baloney. I believe anyone can develop nice hands by working at it, and by riding horses that allow you to have good hands. You can't if you're always riding horses with iron jaws that have learned to stiffen and tighten their neck muscles in resistance to pressure.

11 BASIC POSITION: THE BODY

Your goal is to move as one unit with your horse.

Your seat in the saddle can be considered an extension of your foundation, because without a steady, secure seat, it will be impossible to ride with quiet hands and to keep your upper body stabilized. A rider whose body moves noticeably and who has unsteady hands will never achieve the look of total harmony with his horse.

Remember that in horsemanship, your goal is to move as one unit with your horse. You should blend together and flow together like two Olympic ice skaters in a dance routine.

Achieving a secure seat is one area in which shorter riders, especially shorter-waisted riders, have an advantage over taller riders because their center of gravity is closer to the horse. The closer your center of gravity is to the horse, the eas-

Dameron Allen has excellent body position and balance to communicate and stay in balance with her horse at any gait.

64

Dameron demonstrates the slouched position of some riders. This position puts the majority of the rider's weight behind the motion and directly on the horse's loin, which can cause a sore back.

Compare the rider's head position, eyes, and expression in these two pictures. Above, she is looking down, reflecting a lack of confidence. On the right, her eyes are looking straight ahead, and her expression is alert and reflects a winning attitude. If she were two different riders and you were the judge, who would you pick for first?

ier it is to stay in balance and rhythm with him. A look at professional rodeo cowboys who specialize in bronc and bull riding proves how true this is. The most successful are usually no taller than 5'10". It is extremely unusual for a taller cowboy to excel professionally in the riding events.

Proper seat position means sitting squarely in the middle of the saddle. Although you should be sitting down in the saddle with your weight and balance evenly distributed on each side, you should not be "dead" in the saddle. Your

Todd Bergen is sitting with his upper body behind the motion, and bracing himself in the saddle by jamming his lower legs too far forward.

Here, Todd is sitting correctly and in balance. The difference in his position is reflected by his horse's happier attitude and better motion.

seat muscles should be alive and full of elasticity so you can develop a feel and rhythm with the horse. If you are sitting "dead" you will be jarred every time a hoof hits the ground. Not only will you have no rhythm with the horse, riding won't be much fun.

A fault that some riders have is sitting on their fannies, as if they were in an easy chair. This tends to round the back and shoulders, making the rider appear slumped over, and it also pushes the legs forward. Overall, this makes it difficult to stay in balance with the horse, and to maintain the "wrap" or feel with your legs.

Both your stomach and back should be flat, or straight, your shoulders should be square, and your shoulder blades should be flat. Keeping your shoulders square helps you ride in the middle of your horse. If one shoulder is cocked forward, you'll find yourself "leading" in that direction, instead of sitting straight. And a lot of riders tend to do this with the corresponding shoulder of whichever hand is holding the reins.

When you are "leading" with one shoulder, this puts more weight in that stirrup, and that can make a big difference in how the horse travels. Say, for example, your left shoulder is cocked forward; this puts more weight in your left stirrup. To compensate for this unbalanced weight on his back, the horse will move with his hips going more to the right; it will also cause him to drop his left shoulder, and raise his right shoulder. Both shoulders, of course, should be straight up. All of this makes it more difficult for the horse to travel correctly, and to do such things as change leads.

Your hips should be even in an imaginary vertical line with your shoulders. If you allow the tops of your hips to roll forward, this will put an undesirable arch in your back, and will also ever-so-slightly lift your seat out of the saddle.

From the rear view, the shoulders should be level . . . do not allow one to drop lower than the other. Your head should be straight, and it should be possible to drop an imaginary vertical line from the center rear of your head, down between your shoulder blades, the middle of your waist, the center of the cantle, and the middle of the horse's tail.

If this line is straight as an arrow, it tells the judge you are sitting straight and your saddle is straight. An equitation judge will often position himself so he can study riders as they move toward him and away from him . . . just to see if they are sitting straight, if their stirrups are even, etc.

When a rider tilts or leans to one side, it throws the horse off balance and affects his way of traveling, as we have already talked about. I've seen people who have ridden for years who ride more on one side of their body than the other, and they do not realize it. That's one reason why a horse will often travel better, and do things better going in one direction than the other. You often hear a rider say, for example, that his horse has trouble changing leads to the left, and so the rider continually schools the horse to correct the problem. He generally has little success because, unbeknownst to him, he is causing the problem by sitting unevenly in the saddle.

This problem can also affect rail riders, those who show in such classes as pleasure and horsemanship. I've seen a lot of them whose horses always move better in one direction than the other. Invariably, it is caused by the riders sitting unevenly on their horses.

Some people also have one leg shorter than the other and do not realize it, and this can cause the same kind of problems. They put more weight in the stirrup of the longer leg, and this throws the

Melissa Coffey shows what a typical beginning rider often does; she leans forward, which causes her lower legs to fall back and puts a majority of her weight on the horse's forehand.

Melissa's body and lower leg positions are correct here, but her right arm is too far back, which shifts more of her weight to the left side of the horse.

Dameron's shoulders are square and her back is flat, and her weight is distributed evenly on both sides of the horse. However, her right leg is too far from the horse.

horse off balance.

The position of your head may not seem that important, and it isn't when compared to the correct positioning of the feet, legs, and seat. But nonetheless, head position can enhance or detract from your overall appearance. It should be straight, not tilted, and your eyes should be looking straight ahead, not down at the ground or your horse's neck, or to the side.

Looking down, instead of straight ahead, has several drawbacks. First, you can't see where you are going and if you are doing individual work, your circles will probably be lopsided or egg-shaped, and your run-downs angled instead of straight. Also, you can't tell how far you have travelled in your run-down. You might think you're almost to the fence and had better stop, but in reality you've only gone halfway.

Second, looking down can reflect a lack of confidence to the judge, just as does a person who always looks down when talking.

Third, alternating between looking down and looking up can affect your balance or equilibrium. That's because when you look down, your horse's neck will appear to be stationary while other objects appear to be moving when you look up.

When making run-downs, such as in a reining horse pattern, you should know where you are going to stop, but you should not look at that spot. Look straight ahead at the arena fence, or even at an object outside of the arena. If you look right at the spot where you want to stop, you'll have a tendency to make a short, choppy stop instead of a fluid stop.

Remember to always practice good posture on a horse, but do not confuse

Dameron drops her left shoulder in an exaggerated manner, which causes her to ride with about 80 percent of her weight on the left side. If she actually rode like this, she would probably find that her horse would always move better to the right than to the left.

This is a more subtle example of how some riders unknowingly drop a shoulder (in this case, to the right), and is why many good judges will position themselves so they can view riders from straight behind them.

sitting tall and erect with being stiff. A stiff rider cannot flow with the movement of the horse. I have noticed that there seems to be more stiff riders among the older amateurs. There are almost always sitting correctly, but they have no elasticity of movement. They sit a horse like a bump on a log, and if the horse makes a sudden move, like stumbling or shying, the rider sometimes must grab leather to avoid falling off. A relaxed rider, on the other hand, is more apt to go with the movement of the horse and never lose position.

Remember, too, that good posture is just as important when doing any kind of riding, not just in the show ring when you are being judged. Sitting properly helps the horse regardless of what he is doing, and minimizes the chances of soring his back. It's not unusual to see trail riders hook a leg over the saddle horn, or shift their weight to one side to alleviate their stiffness or soreness. What they don't realize is that this can cause problems to the horse because it intensifies pressure in a particular area of his back.

12 RIDING THE HORSE IN MOTION

Outside of the show ring, it's okay to post the trot, or stand in your stirrups.

Previous chapters have described the rider's ideal position while the horse is standing still. While this position remains relatively the same when the horse is moving, the rider must make subtle changes in order to stay in balance and rhythm with the horse. And the emphasis is on *subtle* changes. A casual observer should not be able to detect any change in the rider's position.

Before going into specifics, however, I want to point out that the basics of good horsemanship are the same regardless of where you are riding. But outside of the show ring, it's okay to deviate from the ideal position that is dictated by rule books.

For example, it's okay to hold the saddle horn. Some beginning western riders are under the impression that it's taboo to ever touch the saddle horn, but that's not true. Horns were originally put on western saddles for a practical reason: as a place to tie or dally a rope when roping cattle. But the horn is also handy for resting your rein hand, grabbing it to prevent a fall, or holding it for balance when clipping along at a brisk trot or hand gallop.

Another example: Rules for western judged events stipulate that the rider must sit the trot. But outside of the show ring, it's okay to post the trot, or stand in your stirrups. A trot is a ground-covering gait that puts less stress on a horse than does a lope or gallop. Trail riders and ranch cowboys use the trot to get somewhere in a hurry, and it's not unusual to see them either posting the trot or standing in their stirrups, sometimes balancing themselves with one hand on the horn.

It's also okay to use two hands on the reins. Here again, some beginning riders believe that when you ride "western," you must only use one hand on the reins, and you must neck-rein the horse. Not true. It's also okay to hold your hands higher or lower than usual, or out to the side, and this is sometimes necessary when training a horse.

The Jog

The western jog, a two-beat diagonal gait, is a slow trot. In fact, the only real difference between a walk and a western jog is that the horse goes from a four-beat gait to a two-beat diagonal gait. Some horses will almost jog slower than they walk. I'm not saying if that's good or bad—only that the jog is not an impulsion gait, as the English trot is, and that it's relatively easy for most riders to sit well, if their horses have a comfortable jog.

Because the jog is so slow, the rider changes his position very little from what it is at the walk. About the only difference is that you don't sit quite as flat in the saddle. Using your muscles, "lift" yourself slightly. This allows you to stay in better balance and timing with the horse, and helps you to absorb the rhythmic movement, especially if the horse has a rough, jarring jog.

The rhythm has a definite beat: one-two, one-two, one-two. This occurs as each diagonal pair of legs (left front/right rear, and right front/left rear)

At the jog, Donna Martinson doesn't change her basic overall position from the walk, except that she isn't sitting quite as flat in the saddle. She's using her muscles to lift herself slightly while feeling the rhythm of the two-beat gait.

move in unison. Counting this beat out loud—"one-two, one-two"—will help you develop the feel of the jog.

Legs are held next to the horse, just so you have very light contact. This increases your feeling of the "inner" horse and what he's doing. Although your legs are not applying any pressure, they are in position to immediately do so when necessary.

Suppose, for example, you feel the horse jogging too slowly, or beginning to fall out of form (becoming "strung out" and needing more collection). The average rider would maintain contact with the mouth while applying leg pressure to move the horse into the bridle. But the really top rider applies this impulsion in rhythm with the jog—when he feels one of the diagonal pairs of legs lifting off the ground to move forward. As you can imagine, there's only a split second when you can do this.

It doesn't matter which pair of legs you time your impulsion with. But if you have trouble getting the feel of when to do it, here's a tip: Apply the leg pressure at the exact time you would be rising out of the saddle if you were posting.

Applying this impulsion with split-second timing is not apparent to anyone watching. But a knowledgeable judge will observe that the horse has eased into a slightly faster jog, or has acquired the needed collection to stay in frame.

Applying leg pressure indiscriminately, or with too much force, can cause the horse to spurt forward, or fall out of form even more.

One problem that some riders acquire at the jog is letting the motion move them from side to side in rhythm with the gait. Left-right, left-right . . . a rider's body moves from side to side. I call this "doing the hula." To correct it, I will have the rider concentrate on the up-down motion instead, as if he were posting. He doesn't actually rise out of the saddle, but he does lift, and then lower, his shoulders and upper body in cadence with the up-down beat of the jog.

By the same token, if a rider has too much bounce at the jog, I'll have him concentrate on the side-to-side motion, and actually do a little bit of the hula to overcome the up-down motion. Gradually he will acquire the happy medium of sitting quietly.

Posting, incidentally, is defined as rising and descending in the saddle in rhythm with the trot. It makes the trot

Your legs should keep a "breathing feel" on the horse.

easier on both horse and rider . . . the rider for obvious reasons, and the horse because it prevents the rider from bouncing on his back. Although posting is not required in western classes, it's handy for anyone to know, especially someone who does a lot of trotting.

Seldom does a judge ask for an extended trot in a western horsemanship class, but it can be called for, so it's good to know what to do. Simply apply more leg pressure while you steady the horse with the reins to prevent him from breaking into a lope. That's probably what he'll do if you haven't ridden him very much at the extended trot, so practice it at home.

Do not post the extended trot. Instead, lift your seat slightly out of the saddle to minimize the impact, and hold your body steady. It's okay to lean slightly forward because this will keep you over the horse's center of gravity.

A judge likes to see a distinct difference between a jog and extended trot, so move your horse out. If he's really rough to ride at the trot, do the best you can—and put a little showmanship into your ride by keeping a pleasant expression on your face. Don't let the judge know how miserable you really are.

The Lope

Because the lope has more impulsion than the jog, it requires more skill and balance to ride properly. Part of this skill is in being able to feel what the horse is doing under you . . . such as whether he's on the correct lead, or if he's lapsing into a four-beat lope. That can happen when he's allowed to lope too slowly or he falls out of frame by becoming strung out behind. The rider then needs to collect him and move him back into a three-beat lope.

At the lope, the disciplined rider keeps his legs and body quiet and relaxed, and moves in rhythm with the horse. To help achieve this rhythm, the rider subtly lifts his body as the horse gathers and lifts himself. The horse "lifts" as his leading

front leg comes off the ground, and that's when the rider should lift. But it's not an actual rising out of the saddle; it's more a matter of thinking "lift."

Something else that will help is letting your hips open and close in rhythm with the three-beat cadence. By this, I mean simply letting your hips move forward and back, but so slightly that it is imperceptible to anyone watching.

Some riders make the mistake of trying to stay with the horse's motion by pumping with their shoulders, which makes them look like a woodpecker at work. If you have this problem, concentrate on keeping your shoulders steady and letting your hips move with the motion. While sitting in a chair and reading this, you probably can't comprehend how your hips move. So next time you're riding, concentrate on how your hips move when the horse lopes. This will give you a better idea of what I mean.

At the lope, you will have more weight in your stirrups than you did at the jog, and your heels will really be down. You will also find it more difficult to keep your legs steady, especially the leg that corresponds to the horse's leading front leg. That leg (yours) will have more of a tendency to swing back and forth than will your other leg. A powerful, long-striding horse also is more difficult to ride with steady legs than a shorter-strided horse that has more collection.

Your legs should also keep what I call a "breathing feel" on the horse. To explain: As the horse's leading front leg comes off the ground, you can feel him gather himself. As he does this, your legs should "breathe in;" as that leg heads back to the ground, your legs "breathe out." Your legs do not actually apply any pressure; it's just a very light contact—so light that that's why I call it a "breathing feel." It will not make the horse go any faster, but it does help keep him in frame (collected) and his back rounded, and it helps you feel what he is doing.

If you are asked to extend the lope,

Unless a rider is really in rhythm with the horse at the lope, and sitting in balance with the horse's equilibrium, the horse cannot use his hocks and his back to move well. In these two pictures, we see Melissa Coffey (top) and Kelly Holder. Melissa demonstrates how some riders lean forward at the lope, while Kelly shows a position that puts her in better balance with her horse.

Todd Bergen is a classic example of a rider sitting out of position in a run-down to make a stop. His legs are too far forward and his upper body too far back, and his shoulders indicate that too much of his weight is on his left side. This causes the horse to stiffen in the poll, drop his shoulders, and move with his hocks way behind him. Notice how his croup is higher than his withers. He's in no position to make a good stop.

apply more leg pressure and keep more contact with the mouth to keep the horse balanced. Stay down in the saddle, let your hips open and close with the motion, and keep your shoulders steady—and your elbows, too!

To see some great examples of how to ride the extended lope and hand gallop, watch the good reining horse riders. They do a beautiful job of keeping their legs and bodies steady, and moving as one with their horses.

Another problem some riders have at the lope is getting ahead of the horse's motion, or behind it. This simply means that you are not in synch with the horse—just as an Olympic ice dancer would not be in synch with her partner if she were a half-step ahead of or behind him.

When the rider is behind the motion, he's always playing catch-up, and this makes it more difficult for the horse to balance himself. The same is true when the rider gets ahead of the motion. When approaching a lead change, for example, the rider will tip or lean forward and "change" before the horse does. Then the horse has to play catch-up, and he cannot make a smooth, fluid change.

Occasionally, a skilled rider in certain circumstances will deliberately ride behind the motion. A good example: When a reining horse is making a run-down, the rider will sit deep in the saddle and drive the horse ahead of him. The deeper he sits and the stronger he uses his legs, the more impulsion he has to drive the horse ahead of him with the speed necessary to make a spectacular, long sliding stop.

Here, Todd is sitting in time and in balance with his horse, who now shows a relaxed poll with his shoulders up. He is also bending in his loins, and driving up under himself so he can get his hocks in the ground to stop. Note that his withers are higher than his loins in this picture.

The Stop

Making a stop from a trot or lope is pretty easy for most riders to manage. Simply move your legs away from the horse, and let your weight settle into the saddle. The important thing is to stop quietly with good form, and to stay in balance with the horse so you do not tip forward, or back.

Stopping a horse from speed, though, separates the really good riders from the "vanilla" riders. The force of the stop can wreak havoc with a rider's position if he does not have a secure, deep seat in the saddle and can't stay in balance with the horse. It's not unusual to see such a rider thrown forward while his feet go out behind him.

Then, of course, there are those riders who deliberately lean way back in the saddle, prop their feet out in front of them, and haul back on the reins. That won't score any points either.

To see some really pretty riders at the stop, again, watch the reiners. They ride through long, powerful stops with seemingly no effort at all, and that's the way it should be.

I teach my riders a one-two-three sequence in making a stop:

1/ Say *whoa.* To the horse, this means "shut 'er down," and he readies his body to stop by dropping his hindquarters and rounding his back.

2/ A split second after saying *whoa,* sit deeper in the saddle. This settling motion serves as a body cue to the horse to stop. Also put more weight into your heels to help steady or brace yourself. This will automatically move your lower legs slightly forward, which will help

What I see here is a rider in total balance and communication with his horse. Without this position, a rider does not have the depth of "feel" needed for athletic stops like this. Note the rider's total extension of his leg and heel, giving him absolute discipline of his seat and legs to ride this horse through the stop in total balance. This is Rocky Dare of Salem, N.J., riding Sure Slide, owned by Clarion Finanz of Zurich, Switzerland.
Photo by Sandy Lee

you stay down in the saddle through the stop.

3/ Apply pressure with the reins. The key here is to start with one pound of pressure, and gradually build to three, four, or five pounds—or whatever it takes to help the horse find his balance in the stop. Sometimes one pound is all that's necessary. Then you set your hand to help keep him stay balanced through the stop.

I always tell my riders to pull on the reins as if they were pulling a carrot out of the ground. If you grab the top of the carrot and jerk, the top will come off. But if you pull gently, the entire carrot will slide easily out of the ground.

It's the same philosophy in stopping a horse. Grab the reins and jerk, and his

head flies up. Take hold of the reins gently and apply gradual pressure, and he settles into the ground in a well-balanced stop.

Once a horse is in the ground and stopping, your hands and body weight help him stay balanced. As soon as he reaches the end of his stop, release the rein pressure instantly and turn loose of his face.

One of the greatest thrills in riding a western horse happens during those few seconds when both you and the horse are totally together in a long, balanced, and graceful stop. Even spectators appreciate it, and that's one reason why reinings are becoming a major spectator event.

I think it's important for a rider to have an overall mental image of a graceful, balanced stop, and to realize that stopping is not a pulling contest. Too many riders try to stop their horses by force. When you do that, three things happen:

1/ The horse braces with his neck and

BILL
GOOLDY

Here is an excellent example of a horse and rider moving in total harmony with each other. This is Jackie Kyle Krshka of Yukon, Okla., riding Sweet Stage, owned by Jack and Sherry Huenergardt of Wichita, Kansas. Jackie reflects total upper body discipline by being able to keep her shoulders square, her back flat, and her body weight evenly distributed in the saddle. This produces a soft, slow hand that communicates with finesse to the horse. This is how you get long sliding stops.
Photo by Bill Gooldy

shoulder muscles, and then his entire body stiffens, he bounces to a stop, and he jars the rider out of the saddle.

2/ It takes a stronger pull every time you stop this horse, because he leans on the bit harder and harder to protect himself.

3/ He begins to dread stopping because he gets hurt every time; therefore he begins trying to stop—called "scotching"—before the rider asks him to, to avoid having his face yanked.

Your approach into the stop should be fluid and effortless—like a feather settling to the ground. That's why giving the verbal cue of *whoa* and the body cue of settling into the saddle are so important. If you just "snatch the horse out of the air" to make him stop, it's impossible for him to do it correctly.

If you and your horse need to practice stopping, you can accomplish a lot from a trot. Put your horse in a long trot along the rail of the arena, or on an outside track, and practice the sequence of saying whoa, sitting down, and picking up the reins (pulling back lightly). This helps both you and your horse with the balance, rhythm, and timing of the stop.

Because the horse is moving slower at a long trot, you have several seconds to do everything correctly, whereas when stopping from speed, you only have a split second. But after you perfect the stop from the long trot, it will be easier to do from speed.

Continually working a horse on stops from speed will burn him out. So work at a trot, and along the rail, or even on a soft dirt road. Don't make stops going down the middle of the arena, as you do in an actual class, because then the horse will begin to anticipate badly. Keep him guessing as to where you might ask him to stop.

Building speed in a turn-around is just like starting your car after you have stopped for a traffic light.

1/ This is a sequence of three turn-around pictures with Todd Bergen. To ask his horse to begin turning, Todd has lifted his rein hand slightly, and to the inside, to turn the nose in the direction of the turn. Todd has also shifted a little more weight to his outside (left) stirrup.

The Turn-Around

In years past, quarter turns and half turns were usually called for in horsemanship classes. But in today's classes that require individual work, riders generally have to make at least one full turn, which is usually referred to as a turn-around, not a spin as it formerly was.

Assuming that the rider has a broke horse that knows how to turn around, there are two important factors in making good ones: proper position of the horse, and proper position of the rider.

To position the horse correctly, lift your hand up and slightly to the inside, to turn the horse's nose slightly to the inside. Do not arc his body too much; you should barely be able to see his inside eye.

To position yourself correctly, shift more of your weight to the outside stirrup than to the inside. If you are turning around to the right, for example, put more weight in your left stirrup. This frees up the right shoulder, in the direction he is turning, so he can turn more easily. Shifting your weight to the inside stirrup can cause him to turn on his front

end instead of on his hindquarters.

The horse's first moves in a turn-around should be slow so you can get the correct positioning. After he makes two or three good cross-overs with his front legs, you can begin clucking to him or use stronger leg pressure to build speed. If you hurry him too fast when you start, you'll jam him and he will lose form.

Building speed in a turn-around is just like starting your car after you have stopped for a traffic light. If you suddenly mash down on the accelerator, the car will lurch forward. But if you ease the car into motion, then accelerate, it will move forward rapidly and smoothly. Use the same technique in making turn-arounds.

Also remember that you teach speed in a turn-around through training, not by neck-reining harder. Applying a neck rein with too much pressure will usually cause the horse to lose form and position, especially if you are riding with a curb bit. The harder you neck rein, the more you pull his nose to the outside, making it difficult for him to turn around properly.

78

2/ The horse still has his pivot foot planted and is crossing over nicely. At this point, Todd is starting to ask for more speed by using more outside leg pressure.

3/ What started out as a nice turn-around is deteriorating because Todd is now reining the horse too hard. This causes the horse to stiffen his body and resist, and lose his position.

13 TRANSITIONS

Smooth transitions require a keen sense of communication between horse and rider.

A transition is the changing from one gait to another, and how a rider and horse make their transitions tells a lot to the judge. An average rider can look pretty good just going along at a walk and jog, and maybe even the lope. But it is the transitions that reveal to the judge the *really good* riders in the class.

The ideal is to change from one gait to the next smoothly, quietly, and efficiently. There should be no perceptible movement or cues given by the rider, and no perceptible change in the horse.

By that I mean he should not reflect anticipation, nervousness, or excitement. One moment he is walking quietly, and the next moment he has moved fluidly into a smooth jog or lope. To do transitions well requires a keen sense of communication between the horse and rider. The horse must be responsive to the rider's cues, and the rider must be able to sense and feel what the horse is doing, or *thinking* about doing.

To go from the walk to a jog is relatively easy, partly because the western

1/ In this sequence of four photos (on four pages), Angie Ross demonstrates the transition from the walk into the lope. Here, the horse is relaxed, yet alert.

2/ Angie takes some of the slack out of the reins, which starts to bring the nose in, and applies subtle leg pressure. Note how the horse's frame is shortening, and how nicely he is responding to Angie's soft hands.

jog is not much faster than a walk. I teach my riders to:

1/ Shorten the reins just a bit to help gather or collect the horse.

2/ Squeeze with both legs to ask for more forward motion. The horse then quietly picks up the jog.

The combination of light contact on the mouth and pressure applied from both of the rider's legs also helps to collect the horse by moving his hindquarters under him, rounding his back, and slightly raising his poll. Some degree of collection is necessary for the horse to move in balance and to make transitions efficiently.

Judges like to see a distinct two-beat gait when the horses are jogging. Some horses jog so slowly they are actually walking with their back legs. This can cost you points in a horsemanship class.

The extended trot is rarely asked for in an equitation or horsemanship class, but if it is, here's what to do. Simply maintain light contact on the mouth so the horse doesn't break into a lope, and increase your leg pressure. Be careful about how much pressure you apply; if it's too much, the horse will probably start loping; if it's not enough, he will not show enough distinction between his jog and extended trot.

To go from the jog or trot back to the

3/ *The horse shows even more collection here. In response to leg pressure, he is rounding his back, allowing him to bring his right hind leg well under him so he can push off into the lope on the right lead.*

walk, check back lightly with the reins, and let your weight settle into the saddle by dropping your hips ever so slightly. It is permissible in the show ring to use a verbal command, such as *whoa* or *walk*, but it should be spoken so only your horse can hear it, not the judge 25 feet away.

To move from the walk into a lope requires more skill, but a good rider on a good horse does it easily. Here's how I teach it . . . and let's assume the rider will ask for the left lead:

1/ Gather up or collect the horse by having light contact with the mouth, and by applying light leg pressure.

2/ Raise your rein hand slightly and move it slightly to the right. This will lift the horse's inside (left) shoulder, making it easier for him to pick up the left lead.

3/ Drop your right hip, by sitting down more on your right seat or "sit-down bone." This helps free up his left hip so his left hind can easily pick up the lead.

4/ Apply pressure from your right leg.

If the horse is trained to pick up either lead, and if you have done your job well, the horse should move quietly into a lope. There's no fuss . . . he doesn't toss his head, open his mouth, lunge sideways, or gallop off. To make the

4/ The horse has moved into the lope softly and fluidly. Although the rider is sitting still, she is not rigid; she's moving in motion with the horse to stay in perfect balance with him.

transition into the lope, it's especially important to use just the right amount of leg pressure. Don't use 20 pounds if you only need 2. That can cause the horse to bolt into the lope, or pick up the wrong lead.

You should be able to immediately tell, through the "seat of your pants," if the horse is on the correct lead. Do not lean over to look at the shoulders. If he's not on the correct lead, do not panic. Bring the horse back to the walk, gather him up, and try it again.

Some riders who start off on the wrong lead will attempt a flying change to the correct lead. This is okay if you are dead-shot sure the horse WILL change leads smoothly and quietly. Otherwise, do not attempt it. To ask for a flying change and have the horse blow it will cost you even more points.

Nor should you angle the horse into the fence and "bounce" him off it in an attempt to force him to change leads. It seldom works, and reflects a lack of training, know-how, and finesse. Even worse, you can disturb other riders.

Although this isn't a training book, I want to mention that the most effective method of cueing a horse for a lead is to use your opposite leg—your right leg to ask for the left lead, and your left leg for

1/ *This is a sequence of five photos (on four pages) showing a change of leads in a western riding pattern. The horse is in the right lead, is collected, and has both shoulders straight up, which is extremely important for changing leads smoothly.*

the right lead. Occasionally, someone will ask me the merits of using a direct-leg cue for the lope—left leg for the left lead, right leg for the right lead.

This is not effective, and not recommended. Why? If the horse does not pick up the left lead, for example, you have no alternative but to apply stronger pressure with your left leg. This will shift his weight to the right, and actually move him to the right. Then it becomes extremely difficult for him to pick up the left lead. On the other hand, applying stronger pressure with your opposite leg helps force him onto the correct lead.

Some riders also feel it is correct to shift their weight into the direction of the desired lead. For a right lead, they shift their weight to the right. Again, this is not effective. Putting more of your weight on the right side makes it more difficult for him to pick up the correct lead, whereas shifting it to the left side frees up his right side, making it easier for him to pick up the right lead.

To get a better idea of how this works, sit up straight in your chair right now, and hold your arms out in front of you. Drop your left shoulder, and now simulate loping in the right lead. Envision

2/ As the horse approaches the marker, Angie collects him even more to prepare him to change leads.

how much more difficult it would be to lope in the right lead if you had extra weight on your right shoulder. That's the problem the horse has if you shift your weight to the right.

Keep in mind that whenever I talk about shifting weight, or dropping your hip to put more weight on your seat bone, these movements are invisible to anyone watching. Only you and your horse realize you are doing it.

What about flying changes of leads? They are required in such classes as reining and western riding, and a judge can ask for them in a horsemanship class. When done properly, a flying change is a fluid movement accomplished with seemingly no effort on the part of horse or rider. Here's how I teach it to my students, assuming they are riding horses trained to make flying changes.

1/ While loping, make sure the horse is collected or gathered up. Do this by shortening the reins to bring his nose in and raise his poll, and by using leg pressure to bring his hindquarters under him. He cannot change leads easily if his head is down, his nose out, and he's strung out behind.

2/ Assuming the horse is on the right lead and I want him to change to the left, I raise my rein hand and move it slightly to the right when I feel his leading leg (right) hit the ground. Raising my hand

3/ As she goes by the marker, she raises her rein hand slightly and moves it to the right to keep both shoulders up.

slightly collects him a bit more, and keeps both shoulders up, and moving it to the right puts his shoulders in line with his rib cage and hips. His body must be in a straight line to change.

3/ At the same time that I raise my rein hand and move it to the right, I shift a little more weight to my right stirrup and squeeze with my right leg to move his hips to the left—and he changes in the very next stride to the left lead.

We previously mentioned how difficult it is for a horse to pick up a lead when a rider has more weight on that side of the horse. This explains why I shift more weight to my right stirrup

when I want to change to the left lead; it "frees up" his left side so he can change more easily.

To change from the left to the right lead, raise your rein hand and move it to the left, shift a little more weight to your left stirrup, and squeeze with your left leg.

When changing leads, continue to sit up straight. Leaning to the inside (the direction to which you are changing) can cause the horse's hindquarters to move to the outside, preventing him from changing leads behind.

Something else we should mention is "cross-firing," which means the horse is

4/ *Immediately after passing the marker, Angie squeezes with her outside (right) leg to move the horse's hip and rib cage over. The horse is just ready to switch leads. Ideally, the horse should change leads a little flatter, but for demonstration purposes, Angie is exaggerating her leg aid to show the change.*

loping with one lead in front, and the other lead behind. For example, he might be on the left lead in front, and the right behind. You can almost immediately tell when the horse is cross-firing because his gait will be so rough.

It's not unusual for a young, or a not-well-trained horse, to do this. He will pick up the correct lead in front, and the incorrect behind. It also happens, not infrequently, when a rider asks for a flying change of leads; the horse changes in front, but not behind. If this happens to you in a horsemanship class, bring the horse back to a walk, and start over. If you are doing a figure-eight, it would be

5/ *Here, he has changed to the left lead, both front and behind, and continues loping quietly.*

1/ In this photo sequence, Angie demonstrates dropping from the lope to the walk. Here, she is sitting in excellent balance and has nice contact with the mouth.

2/ Now she's sitting a little deeper in the saddle, is putting more weight into her heels, and has moved her shoulders slightly back. Ideally, the rider should not lean back this much. On the other hand, her body shows a suppleness in her transitions, which is important.

3/ As her horse slows, Angie maintains her balance and position.

4/ Almost down to the walk. This sequence is an excellent example of slowing to the walk with almost no visible cues, while continuing to sit in rhythm and balance with the horse.

If a judge sees you angle a horse into the fence to help make him pick up the correct lead, he will count off for it. On the other hand, it won't cost you as many points as keeping your horse straight, but picking up the incorrect lead. The angle shown in the right picture is more subtle.

best to ease down to a trot, and then pick up the lope again. Simply applying stronger pressure from your outside leg might not work, and could cause him to jet through the rest of the figure-eight too fast.

To go from the lope back to the walk, check the horse lightly with the reins, and drop your hips to settle down into the saddle. Do not lean back, or sit with your weight dead in the saddle. You can also say *whoa* or *walk*.

Use just the right amount of pressure on the reins. Too much, and the horse might throw his head and open his mouth. Too little and you won't get stopped.

Another question I'm sometimes asked is whether spurs should be used by equitation riders. I usually say yes—if the rider knows how to use spurs correctly. The rider should first ask the horse by applying leg pressure; if the horse doesn't respond, then the rider should lightly apply the spur. If the spur is applied without any warning, the horse will become tense and jumpy, and might start wringing or popping his tail

At the extended trot, Kelly Holder maintains light contact with the mouth to prevent the horse from breaking into a lope.

every time the spur touches him.

At one of my recent clinics, a teen-age girl was riding a rather nice horse, but she had no patience with him. Every time she needed to apply a leg cue, she spurred first, and rather vigorously. It was a classic example of a spur being used incorrectly, and the horse's attitude began to reflect it.

I do not recommend spurs when a rider has not yet developed a secure seat in the saddle. Whenever that rider loses his balance, he will accidentally poke the horse with the spurs. Nor should spurs be used by a very young rider whose legs do not hang below the horse's barrel, unless he's riding a plumb lazy horse who doesn't object to always being poked by the spurs.

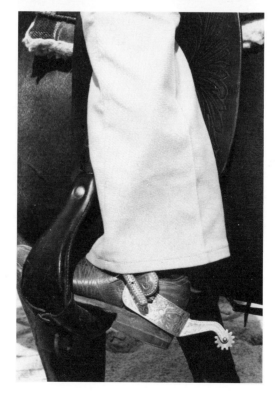

Spurs are okay for equitation riders if the rider knows how to use them correctly.

14 INDIVIDUAL TESTS

Some associations spell out exactly what the judge can call for.

In many horsemanship and equitation classes today, riders are required to work individually as well as on the rail. Some associations, such as the AHSA, spell out exactly what the judge can call for, while in other associations, it's optional with the individual judge. Always know the rules under which a show will be judged so you are prepared.

At smaller shows, you probably will not be challenged with as difficult a test as you would at the Quarter Horse Congress for example, or in an AHSA stock

seat medal class. The age group of the class also plays a role. Older age groups should be required to do more difficult tests than the 11-and-unders.

In shows approved by the American Horse Shows Association, here is a list of tests from which judges must choose:

1/ Individual performance on the rail.

2/ Figure eight at the jog.

3/ Lope and stop.

4/ Figure eight at lope on correct lead, demonstrating simple change of lead. (This is a change whereby the horse is

When the rider's body is opposite the marker, that's when the required maneuver should be executed, whether it's stopping, picking up the lope, or whatever.

A simple test is asking each rider to back up, individually. Generally when it's a female rider, the judge tips his hat.

Loping on a straight line between the two circles in a figure eight.

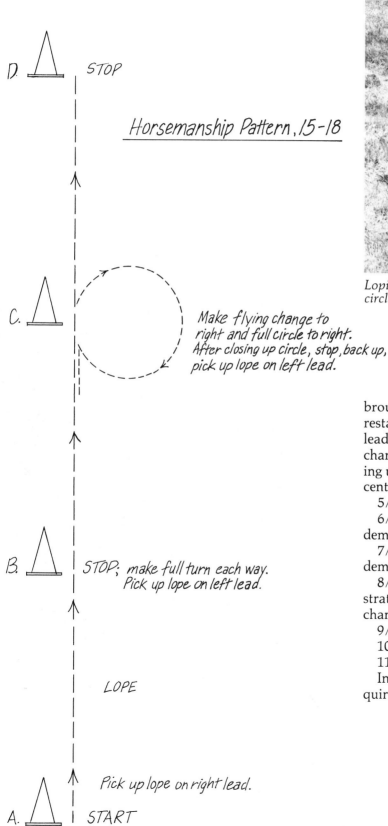

D. STOP

Horsemanship Pattern, 15-18

C. Make flying change to right and full circle to right. After closing up circle, stop, back up, pick up lope on left lead.

B. STOP; make full turn each way. Pick up lope on left lead.

LOPE

A. Pick up lope on right lead.

START

brought back to the walk or jog and restarted into a lope on the opposite lead.) One figure eight demonstrates two changes of lead and is completed by closing up the last circle and stopping in the center of the eight.

5/ Ride without stirrups.

6/ Figure eight at lope on correct lead, demonstrating flying change of lead.

7/ Change leads down center of ring, demonstrating simple change of lead.

8/ Ride serpentine course, demonstrating flying change of lead at each change of direction.

9/ Demonstrate sliding stop.

10/ Execute 360-degree turns (spins).

11/ Roll-backs.

In many instances, the judge is required to post the individual pattern for

To me, proper circles show as much fluidness, smoothness, and horsemanship as do stops and turn-arounds.

In this test, the rider approached the marker at a trot. . . .

a horsemanship class at least one hour before the class, and this is a big help to riders.

Most AQHA shows like to keep individual patterns to 30 seconds or less since these shows generally run so long. With a time limit like this, I'll ask for a pattern that demonstrates a couple of transitions so I can see how light a rider's hands are, and how he uses his legs and other aids and communicates with his horse.

I might also ask for one or two circles to see if the rider can arc the horse correctly around his (the rider's) inside leg; to see if the rider moves in balance and rhythm with the horse, or if he just jams him around; and to see if the rider's rein hand is steady. It must be in order for the horse to follow the inside rein and arc correctly. When a rider is circling, I can also tell if the rider is ahead of or behind the motion of the horse.

To me, proper circles show as much fluidness, smoothness, and horsemanship as do stops and turn-arounds, but I wouldn't have said that earlier in my judging career. In past years, many horsemen thought circles were only a means to show a change of leads, and the circles themselves were never judged. But now, with judging being far more

. . . She stops at the marker and then side-passes to the left. . . .

. . . And lopes off in the right lead. She did a nice job.

In individual tests, I almost always ask for a stop because this reveals so many things about a rider. In this set of pictures, the rider makes a nice, balanced stop, with his rein hand not seeming to move.

In these two pictures, the rider is making a nice approach to the judge, but then he blows it by leaning back and raising his hands far too high.

The sequence of five photos on these two pages depicts a test I often ask of riders in older age groups. Each rider jogs or lopes to the marker, stops, makes a full turn, and then lopes off in a designated lead. This test reveals a lot about a rider's hands; all too often I see riders getting too strong with their hands, especially in the turn-around, causing their horses to fall out of position.

intensive, circles receive as much attention as any other movement.

Circles must be done precisely, and they must be perfectly round, not egg-shaped or banana-shaped. Lead changes must be executed in an exact location, and the horse must have the correct arc and be moving in a steady cadence. It takes a skillful rider to do this.

I almost always ask for a stop because this reveals several things, such as how soft and slow the rider's hands are, and how much control he has over his own body. If the rider has quick hands, it will show when the horse flips his head up

The rider must be able to control his body so the stop doesn't bounce him out of the saddle.

and gets stiff in the poll. As I've already mentioned, I like to see a rider take hold of the mouth as if he were pulling a carrot out of the ground; he should take hold softly, with a gradual pull.

The rider must also be able to control his body so that when the horse stops, the rider isn't bounced out of the saddle.

Turn-arounds or spins show me how much control a rider has over his horse, if he can use his hands and legs correctly, and if he's in balance with the horse. If he's over-riding the horse (using too much leg and rein pressure), I can tell because the horse will turn in the middle

or on his forehand, not on his hindquarters. If he's under-riding, the horse won't have enough impulsion to make a full 360-degree turn and will fizzle out.

One thing I've noticed among riders doing individual patterns is that the really super rider gets better the farther he goes, and he's riding his best at the end of the pattern. For example, suppose the pattern calls for one figure eight with two changes, followed by a stop and a full turn. When the rider gets to the full turn, he will really burn it because he has gradually built to it with rhythm, feel, and balance on his horse.

The biggest problem I see in horsemanship classes is riders getting in too big a hurry—they are too strong with their legs, too quick with the hands, and they are too demanding. This causes their horses to over-react.

In the 1960s and early '70s, if a rider could stay on pattern, get his lead changes, and make a decent stop, he could probably win the class, but not

Round, smooth, and clean circles do not just happen—they are created by the rider, as shown in this sequence of four photos with Todd Bergen. Todd is in total harmony with his horse because of his correct position and balance, which lets his rein hand remain steady and slow, which, in turn, keeps the horse's shoulders up and creates the proper arc. I particularly like the last photo because it shows the correct arc; the rider should only be able to see the tip of the nose and the corner of the inside eye. Note also the relaxed attitude of the horse.

anymore. Today, most judges will give more points to riders whose horses work correctly with soft polls, closed mouths, and relaxed and supple bodies than they will to riders who might have more flash, but whose maneuvers are stiff and jerky. I certainly will.

I like to see a rider who communicates softly with his horse. My pet peeve is the rider who continually jerks at his horse . . . he's always picking on him. A lot of kids and adults do this and don't even realize it. Whenever I see it, I get a real negative attitude toward that rider.

Another problem: making the required maneuver at the precise location specified by the judge. For example, suppose the rider should pick up the lope at marker C. When the rider's body is opposite the marker, that's when the horse should pick up the lope. This means that the rider must *prepare* the horse to pick up the lope *before* reaching the marker; waiting *until* you reach the marker will mean you are beyond it when the horse actually lopes. That will cost you points.

Remembering a pattern is a problem for both youngsters and adults, whether

My pet peeve is the rider who continually jerks at his horse.

This picture shows, without question, what happens when the rider throws his weight to the inside of his circles. The horse is resisting the motion by sticking his nose to the outside of the circle, dropping his inside (right) shoulder, and letting his hips drift to the outside of the circle.

it's in a horsemanship class or reining class. To remedy this, I suggest to my riders with this problem that they walk the pattern on foot, outside of the arena. Or, that they go into the arena during the lunch break or before the show starts and walk the pattern. That also allows you to check for bad footing.

At home, you can walk through the standard reining patterns until you know them by heart, and you can also ride through them on a practice horse. Do not use the horse you will actually be showing because he will learn the pattern as well as you, and that will cause him to start anticipating lead changes, stops, etc. Working him repeatedly on patterns will also cause him to sour out and express his displeasure by wringing his tail, pinning his ears, and perhaps balking at entering the arena.

What impresses me more than anything else in a horsemanship class is a rider's total communication with the horse, his balance, and his ability to use his aids well. I also like to see a rider who uses his eyes well, reflects confidence, and who has the look that says, "I will do a better job than anybody else in this class."

Sample Patterns

For Riders 11 & Under:
   1/ Walk from A to B.
   2/ Jog from B to C.
   3/ Pick up lope on left lead at C.
   4/ At D, stop and back.

For Riders 12-14:
   1/ Lope from A to B on right lead.
   2/ Stop at B; side-pass to the right for five feet.
   3/ Pick up lope on left lead.
   4/ Stop and back at C.

102

The camera caught Todd changing leads in these two photos. His horse is making a flat, quiet, non-resistant, balanced change in the left photo. But in the right photo, Todd demonstrates throwing his weight to the inside, looking down at the ground, and over-using his hand—all of which causes the horse to make a rough, hopping change. Looking down can also cause a rider to lose his equilibrium and his perspective of where he is in his circles.

For Riders 15-18:

1/ Lope from A to B on right lead.

2/ Stop at B; do a full turn each way.

3/ Lope on left lead to C.

4/ At C, make flying change to right and full circle to right.

5/ After closing up circle, stop, back up, immediately pick up lope on left lead.

6/ Stop at marker D.

In classes where individual patterns are not required, I will sometimes have riders do simple tests out of the line-up. For example, I can ask a rider to:

1/ Back up several feet, then jog forward into line-up.

2/ Walk forward, make one full turn to right; back into line-up.

3/ Walk forward five feet; stop; pick up lope on right lead; lope around the end of the line-up and return to your original position.

15 EXERCISES

Exercises can make good riders out of beginners in a relatively short time.

There are a number of exercises a rider can do to improve his balance and timing, to develop his lower legs so he can use them more effectively, to develop a more secure seat, and to achieve better hands. I especially like beginning riders to do these exercises because I can make *good* riders out of them in a relatively short time.

For example, I can take someone who has never been on a horse, have him do these exercises in twice-a-week lessons, and in three weeks he will have good balance on almost any horse. If I were to take this same person and give him the traditional lessons, we're talking three months.

People who already know how to ride—even good riders—can benefit greatly from these lessons, too. Someone, for example, whose feet tend to float in the stirrups, or whose hands are unsteady and continually bump or jerk the horse's mouth, or who cannot stay down in the saddle when the horse stops, or who cannot develop a rhythm on the horse, or who . . . and the list is endless.

Another great thing about these exercises: You don't need an instructor telling you what to do. You can do some of them by yourself . . . and they're fun, too.

Lower Leg Control

In my teaching, I often use the term "organized and disciplined legs." This means legs that are quiet—they stay in one place instead of moving back and forth. This also means legs that can apply one ounce of pressure or ten pounds, whatever the situation calls for. To de-

Dameron Allen demonstrates an excellent exercise to develop lower leg control: Put your hands behind your back and lean over and touch your nose on the horse's neck. Do not let your lower legs move.

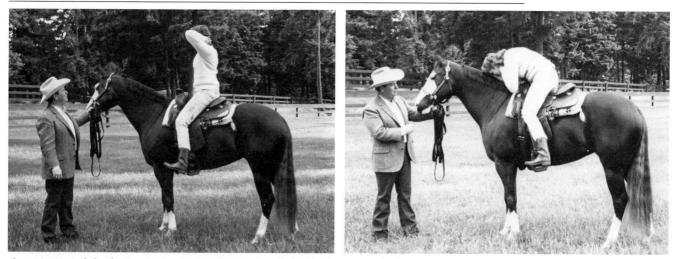

A variation of the first exercise is to put your hands behind your neck. Leaning over is more difficult to do with your hands behind your neck.

Touching one toe with your opposite hand is a stretching and leg-control exercise. Again, do not let your legs move.

velop this kind of leg control, there are several beneficial exercises:

1/ While sitting on your horse, put your hands behind your back, and bend over and touch your nose on the horse's neck 25 times. Take your feet out of the stirrups, and keep your legs steady. As you lean forward, the natural tendency is for your legs to move behind you; do not let this happen. Repeat this exercise in segments of 25 until you can do 100 non-stop.

2/ This exercise is almost the same as #1 but put your hands behind your neck instead of your back. In addition to improving your leg control, this develops your back muscles, and helps improve muscle tone through the hips and seat.

3/ Put both hands straight out to the side, and do a repetition of touching your left toe with your left hand, and your right toe with your right hand. Keep your legs in the correct position, your shoulders square, and your back as straight as possible. This is a muscle stretching and toning exercise.

4/ This is a variation of #3, in which you touch your left toe with your right hand, and your right toe with your left hand. Again, concentrate on keeping your legs in the correct position. This exercise develops more leg control, and will help a rider who tends to lean to one side. For example, if he rides more to the left side, I'll have him touch his right toe with his left hand 20 or 30 more times to develop the left side of his body.

105

The second level of this exercise is to fold your arms across your chest and post to the trot.

Posting at the trot with your hands stretched straight up is the most difficult exercise of these three.

Heels-Down Exercise

If you cannot ride with your heels lower than your toes, you cannot use your legs effectively. To see what I mean, sit up straight in your chair, right now while you are reading this (sit in a straight-back chair, not an easy chair). Leaving your toes on the floor, draw your heels up, and move your legs in, as if you were applying pressure to a horse. See how weak and ineffective your legs are?

Now put your heels on the floor and bring your toes up . . . and simulate applying pressure. Your legs should be much stronger and more effective.

When your heels are up, you have no power in your legs because the leg muscles are contracted. Besides that, it tends to tilt your shoulders forward, making you look like a monkey on a football. With your leg muscles extended, you have power in your legs. That's why every horsemanship book ever written says to keep your heels lower than your toes.

The leg exercises already described will strengthen your legs, enabling you to do a better job of keeping your heels down. But if you are still having trouble, try this:

While you are riding, put your heels in the *front* of your stirrups (you should, of course, be riding with boots) and stand up in the stirrups. After you get the hang of this at the walk, try it at the jog. No fair hanging on to the saddle horn! Next, try posting at a slow trot. Finally, do it at the lope.

When you first start doing this, two minutes will be about as long as you can manage. But practice until you can build to 15 minutes. I guarantee you that within two weeks, you will find it much easier to keep your heels down.

Seat, Balance, and Timing Exercises

The really good rider has a seat that is totally independent of his hands. In other words, his seat is so secure in the saddle that he does not have to hang on to the reins to maintain his balance, a common fault among beginning and novice riders. As we've said before, for the horse to work with a steady head and quiet mouth, the rider's hands must be quiet . . . not continually moving around and bumping the mouth.

Watch the top riders; regardless of whether they are in the show ring, the cutting pen, or on the ranch, their hands never move despite how fast the horses might be moving, or turning.

The following exercises will help develop a more secure seat, as well as improve your balance and timing, which are an integral part of having a good seat. It's best to do these exercises in a round corral with a ground man controlling the horse on a longe line. That's because the rider cannot do most of them and also hold the reins. However, if a rider has no help, he can do them in a round corral on a quiet, reliable horse by using closed reins and looping them over the saddle horn.

1/ Fold your arms across your chest, put the horse in a trot, and stand up in the stirrups for a count of ten, then sit for ten. Next, stand for a count of nine, sit for nine; stand for eight, sit for eight. Continue until you are posting every other stride. Then repeat the entire process *without* stirrups.

When a rider can do this well, I will have him pick up his stirrups and stand for two strides, sit for two strides; stand for two, sit for two. The rider should

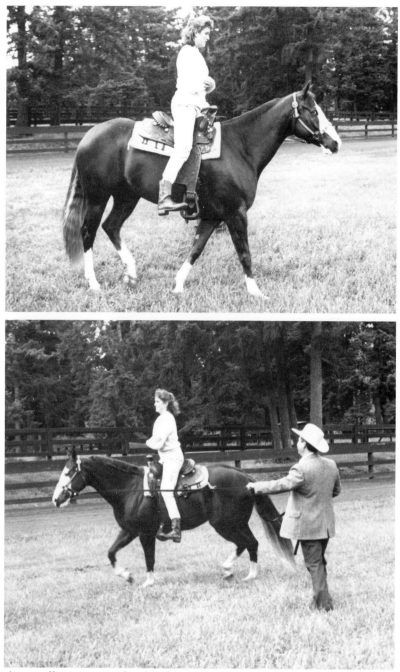

An excellent exercise for developing a more secure seat is to fold your arms across your chest and stand up for a count of ten, then nine, etc. Do this first with stirrups, then without.

count to himself, "Stand one-two, sit one-two; stand one-two, sit one-two." This same exercise should be repeated without stirrups, and in variations—such as standing for three counts, sitting for three; or standing for four and sitting for five, etc.

Whenever you are sitting for the required count, tuck your fanny under you and push the horse with your seat bones, as if you are trying to drive him forward by pushing on him.

This exercise does a couple of things.

107

Here's a good exercise for improving your timing and balance. Hold your arms straight out and turn your body in rhythm with the horse's stride. Dameron is turning to the left when the left front foot moves forward.

First, it helps the rider develop an incredible balance and rhythm with the horse, an absolute necessity to having a secure seat. Second, pushing with your seat bones for the "down count" develops a snugger seat so you aren't just merely floating in the saddle.

The ability to sit down in the saddle and drive the horse with your seat and legs increases your control of the horse—to maintain his impulsion, to keep him collected, to keep him moving in a good three-beat lope, to keep him circling correctly, to keep him in the ground in a stop, and so forth.

A rider who does not have this seat and leg control will try to use his upper body (by leaning forward) to make the horse move on. This means little to the horse because the upper body has no contact with the horse. Also, when the upper body leans forward, the legs usually go back; then the rider cannot use his legs at all, he gets ahead of the horse's motion, and the horse usually loses his impulsion.

2/ With the ground man still handling the longe line, put the horse in a trot. Hold your arms straight out to the side and turn your upper body first to the left, then to the right, in rhythm with the horse. That is, when you feel his right front foot coming down, turn to the right so you are actually looking at a 90-degree angle to the right. When the left front foot is coming down, turn at a 90-degree angle to the left.

When you can do this well with stirrups, then drop your stirrups and do it without them.

In addition to improving your timing and balance, this exercise makes you sit in the middle of the horse because if you are off to one side, you cannot turn without danger of falling off. It also tones the muscles in the middle of your back and your shoulders.

3/ With the horse at a lope and your feet in the stirrups, put your hands behind your neck. If the horse is in the left lead, bring your left shoulder forward, then back, as the left shoulder of the horse moves forward and back. Do the same with your right shoulder when the horse is in the right lead. This exercise helps develop timing and rhythm.

4/ This exercise is done at the trot, with your feet in the stirrups, and both

108

arms held straight out to the side. Move both arms simultaneously in small circles in cadence with the trot. To be more specific, if the horse is moving to the left, start each circle as you feel the right front leg coming off the ground; this would be the same time you would be rising out of the saddle if you were posting the right diagonal.

When the horse is trotting to the right, start each circle as you feel the left front leg coming off the ground—as if you were posting the left diagonal. This exercise helps develop timing as well as coordination of your entire body. It also gives you a tremendous feeling for what the horse is doing under you.

5/ This one involves posting at the trot without stirrups, with your hands straight out in front of you. You can do this first with stirrups, then without. Move each hand up and down in rhythm with the horse's trot and your posting. For example, as the horse's left shoulder is moving forward, you should be rising out of the saddle, and your left hand should be going up.

With the horse at the lope, put your hands behind your neck. If the horse is in the left lead, move your left shoulder forward and back in unison with the horse's left shoulder. This exercise develops timing and rhythm.

Here's another timing exercise. At the trot, hold your arms straight out and move them in a circular motion, making one complete circle with each stride.

To build confidence in a beginning rider, I will ask her to do what we call the "around-the-world exercise." With your arms straight out, turn completely around on the horse, without touching horse or saddle. (Be sure to use a gentle horse.)

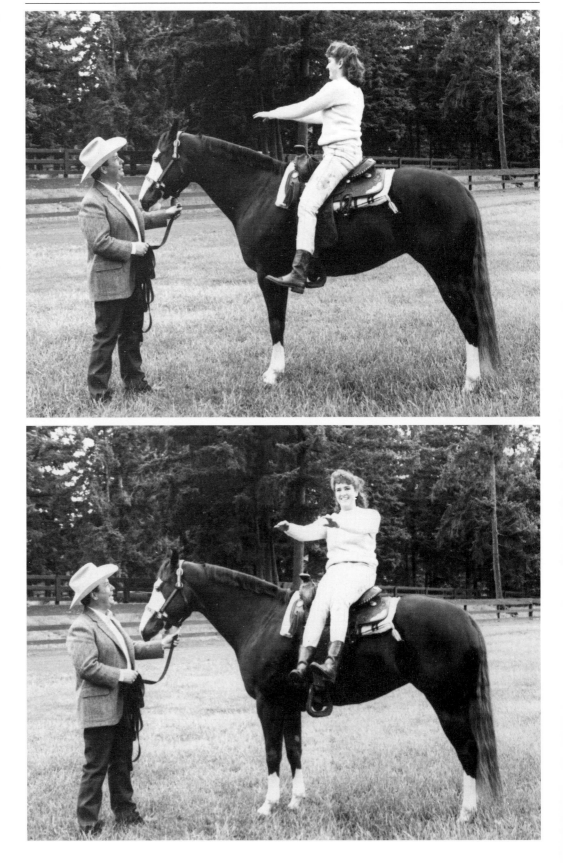

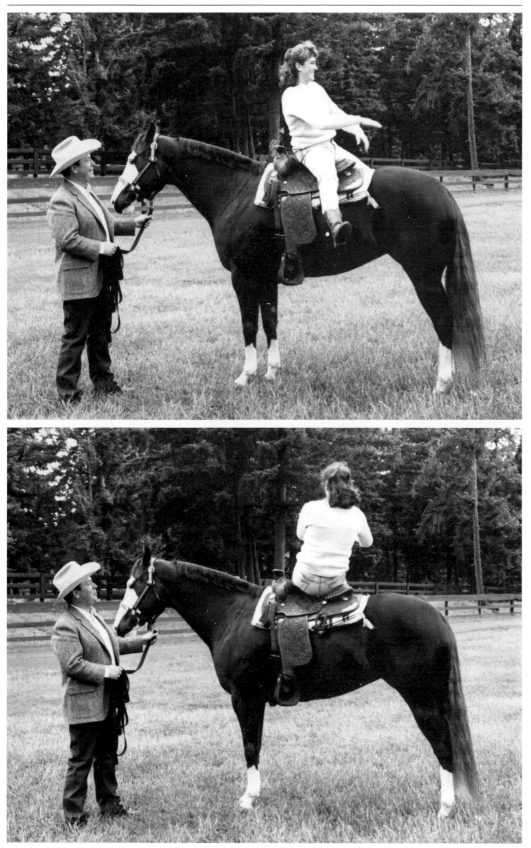

If the rider happens to slide off, he finds out it's no big deal (usually), and that builds his confidence.

As a test to see if you have light hands, attach the reins to the bit with a strand of mane or tail hair, or thread. Do this only on a broke horse in an enclosed area.

6/ I sometimes work my more advanced riders in a round corral without a longe line, on a reliable horse that I can roll back into the fence by using a longe whip. The horse has first been taught this without a rider; all I have to do is step in the direction the horse is going and pop the whip in front of him. I do not hit the horse. The horse also responds to verbal commands, especially *whoa*.

The rider sits with arms folded across his chest. Initially, the horse trots while the rider posts with and without stirrups. Then the rider moves the horse into a lope and I periodically roll the horse back into the fence.

Anyone who thinks he's a good rider should try this. As the horse rolls back, the rider has to stay screwed down in the saddle because there is nothing to hold on to. Consequently, this is a tremendous exercise for developing balance and a secure seat.

Do it only in a controlled situation, however, with a reliable horse and a knowledgeable ground person.

7/ This is another exercise I do with more experienced riders. I blindfold them, and work the horse on a longe line. If a rider has had trouble developing a feel for what the horse is doing, this exercise is a great help.

Confidence Exercise

Some beginning riders are simply afraid of being on a horse. To build their confidence, I will have someone hold the horse and have the rider sit sideways on the horse. When the rider relaxes, I ask him to move back into the correct position. This is repeated until the rider has the confidence to sit backwards . . . and then eventually make a complete circle on the horse.

If he happens to slide off, he finds out it's no big deal (usually), and that builds his confidence even more.

Here is a fun test for more experienced riders: Put your arms straight out to the side, and make a complete circle on the horse without grabbing leather.

Eye Exercise

Beginning riders have a tendency to always look down at the neck. To overcome this habit, pick out an object in the ring, or even outside of the ring, and keep your eyes fixed on it while the horse moves in different directions. Or pick out several objects and move your eyes back and forth between them regardless of the direction in which your horse is going. This will also help you develop a better feel for your horse.

Hands

The old saying "light hands mean a light mouth" is so true, and here are several exercises to see just how light your hands are—and to improve them if need be.

1/ Hold a full glass of water in one hand while you ride your horse at the various gaits, including reverses and circles. Obviously, if you have quick, jerky hands, you're going to get the horse and your pant leg wet.

2/ Ride your horse with a piece of thread tied between each rein and the bit . . . or use several strands of mane or tail hair, as the old-time vaqueros did. Obviously, if you can ride without breaking the thread, you have pretty good hands, and your horse has a light, well-developed mouth. Do this test only in a confined area, such as a round corral, and preferably only on a well-broke horse. If you keep breaking the thread at a walk and jog, don't lope.

3/ Put a snaffle bridle on the horse. While he is standing quietly, take the left rein and slowly tighten it to bring the horse's nose back to the left stirrup. When the nose gets there, drop the rein, and repeat the same procedure with the right rein.

This is a lateral flexion test for the horse, and it helps you develop a feel for how hard you are pulling on the reins. If the horse throws his head and resists, you are pulling too hard or he doesn't know how to respond correctly. If his nose doesn't come, you are pulling too softly.

4/ This exercise helps you get a better feel of how to handle, or manipulate the reins, and you don't need a horse for it. You can even do it in the living room while watching television. Hang your bridle on a chair in front of you, as if it were on a horse. Practice taking up on

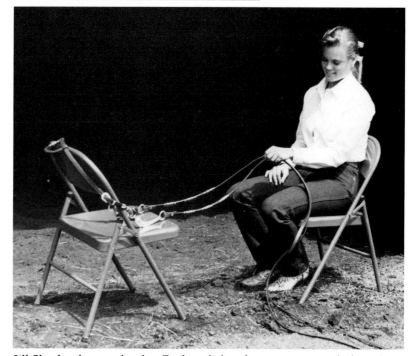

Jill Shrake shows what her Dad made her do every evening before she could have dinner. This exercise helped her develop a better feel for lengthening and shortening the reins.

the reins, and loosening them. This is an especially good exercise if you ride with split reins.

Summary

When we go out to ride, we all have a tendency just to get on our horses and go, but exercises should become a part of our everyday routine. Other athletes always warm up with a series of exercises, and riders should be no different. You don't have to do all of the exercises we have described every day, but spend five or ten minutes doing several of them. And alternate which ones you use. You will be surprised at how your riding skills will gradually improve with a daily few minutes of exercises.

16 PSYCHOLOGY

Mental preparation is almost as important as physical preparation.

In today's athletic world, sports psychology is playing an increasingly important role, whether it's in track and field events, tennis, ice-skating, football, the rodeo arena, the horse show ring, and so forth. This is because both coaches and competitors are learning that mental preparation is almost as important as physical preparation.

Several years ago, for example, a study was done with a group of 100 track and field athletes. They were divided into 4 groups of 25 each, and their training regime went like this:

Group 1: Physically train for six hours daily.

Group 2: Physically train for five hours daily; spend one hour mentally thinking about their event— the correct form to use, how to improve themselves, etc.

Group 3: Physically train for three hours daily; mentally prepare themselves three hours daily.

Group 4: Physically train two hours daily; work on mentally getting ready four hours daily.

Before a class, I will discuss with a student exactly how he or she should ride the class, especially if individual patterns are to be ridden.

114

Thirty days later, in competition, the group that did significantly better was the last group—the one that spent only two hours daily in physical training, but four hours a day in mental preparation.

This is an excellent example of how important mental preparation is, yet it is a relatively new concept in the horse show world.

I want to stress, however, that mental preparation does not mean saying to yourself, "I am going to be a world champion," or "I am going to win the all-around next weekend." All that does is inflate your ego, and will hurt you a lot more than it will help you.

What it does mean is to mentally picture yourself as you compete in each event. Fix the image in your mind of just how you will go through a horsemanship pattern, for example. Do it perfectly. Mentally review just how you will ask the horse to make his transitions, change leads, and stop. If it's a trail class, picture how you will approach and negotiate each obstacle. If it's a reining class, go through the pattern, reviewing how you will make your circles, and the 1-2-3 procedure in asking for a lead change, or a spin, or a stop.

Feel yourself moving his shoulder over and putting more weight in your outside stirrup as you ask him to change leads. See yourself backing up quickly and in a straight line. If you will be going into showmanship, picture your horse working to perfection.

These mental exercises are also a great help if you find yourself getting nervous the night before the show. Sit down, relax, and mentally go through your classes for the next day. It's amazing how it will help.

A marvelous example of how mental preparation can help occurred at one of my clinics. A girl named Cathy Christianson attended who had an old horse that just couldn't do anything, and she was riding a bareback pad to boot. Consequently she spent most of her time just doing exercises in the round corral, and listening as I worked with the other riders on their own horses because she wasn't advanced enough to work with the rest of the group.

On the last day, I brought a reining

Alicia Pershern of Elmira, Ore., and her Quarter Horse, King Rojo Bill, at the 1986 Oregon State Fair where Alicia won the amateur western horsemanship. A former student of mine, Alicia was the reserve champion in western horsemanship at the 1982 AJQHA World Championship Show in Tulsa and reserve champion in amateur western horsemanship at the 1986 AQHA World Championship Show.

horse for some of the kids to ride and get the feel of stops and turn-arounds. Even though this horse was burned out, he could still do a nice job. Cathy kept pestering me to let her ride the reining horse, so I finally said okay. Keep in mind that Cathy was just a beginner.

I put her on the horse and told her to lope him a few minutes to get the feel of him, then gallop him down the arena, and mentally go through the 1-2-3 process of asking him to stop. Well, she galloped him down the arena, did the 1-2-3 and said whoa, and this horse just melted into the ground. I thought she was just lucky, so I had her do it again— three more times, and the horse just kept stopping better and better.

So then I told her to lope across the arena and change leads, using the procedure I had taught the other kids. Well, she did it perfectly . . . the horse never changed leads better in his life. Okay, turn him around, I told her, and he darn near threw her off he spun so fast.

What had happened? Cathy had the chance all week to study the other riders, and absorb what I was telling them. She

Kanoe Durdan Spear, Sisters, Ore., rode with me for nine years and competed successfully in a variety of classes, including trail, horsemanship, pleasure, and cowhorse. She's shown here on Flag Bar at a Junior Cow Palace show in San Francisco. **Photo by Fallaw**

The more you worry about something, the greater the chance that your horse will blow it.

was observant, remembered what she had heard, and went over in her mind the process of making a horse change leads, stop, turn around, and so forth. She mentally reviewed everything she learned when she finally got on a horse that could do these things, and she did a fabulous job.

Later, Cathy's dad bought her a much better horse, and her riding and showing progressed to the point that she entered the trail horse competition one year at the Cow Palace in San Francisco. Her mental preparation and positive outlook helped her negotiate one obstacle that almost everybody else had trouble with.

The obstacle was a tire, and horses were supposed to trot through it. Well, practically all the riders stopped and then stepped through it . . . but Cathy had her horse trot right through it, and did a beautiful job.

I asked her later how she managed to do it when no one else did. She replied, "First, I knew my horse would do it; and second, I imagined myself putting my own foot in the tire when we approached it, and he just stepped right into it."

That's the power of positive thinking. If she had worried that the horse wouldn't step into it, he probably wouldn't have. The more you worry about something, the greater the chance that your horse will blow it. Never have negative thoughts before a class; mentally go through the process of what you will be required to do, and then picture the horse doing it perfectly.

A classic example of how negative thinking works happened to one of my students at the AJQHA Finals in Tulsa several years ago. This girl was a superstar, and had won several dozen all-arounds at AQHA youth shows. In the qualifying round for horsemanship at Tulsa, she placed first by four points. She was a lead-pipe cinch to win the world championship.

On the day of the finals, about ten minutes before the class, we went over the pattern that would be used. She knew it by heart, and knew just what she had to do. Then, being the proud coach of the next world champion, I puffed up and walked around talking with everybody.

About two minutes before the class, this girl's mother came down out of the stands and told her, "Whatever you do, don't let your horse drop a hind lead change for a couple of strides like he did at Eugene two weeks ago . . . because this is almost the same pattern."

Well, the rider went into the ring, let the horse drop his shoulder, and he missed his hind lead change for two strides. Obviously she didn't win the world championship. The mother didn't realize what she had done, and I was just as guilty for not staying with the girl. If I had, I could have stopped her mom from planting such a negative thought immediately before the class.

Negative thoughts can have bad effects in all walks of our life. For example, I know a minister who counsels prisoners. Of the prisoners he has worked with, 95 percent were told at some time by their parents that they were so bad they would end up in prison. And they did. These men never received any positive input from their parents, only negative.

The same thing applies in our teaching and training, and I've done one experiment that proves it. At a clinic, I'll randomly split the riders into two groups. As the first group prepares to ride the final test, I'll say to them: "It's been a pleasure to work with you because you have ridden so well and have shown marked improvement. You are handling your horses well, keeping your hands soft and slow, you are sitting in the middle of your horses, and I've hardly seen you make any mistakes. It's exciting to work with people who do this well." Then I have them go through the pattern.

The second group, I'll say something like, "I know this pattern is too hard for you because you have been making mistakes all morning. Your timing is off, your rhythm is off, and your hands are harsh and jerky. I should have selected an easier pattern for you, but go ahead and do this one."

I've done this experiment about 20 times, and *always*, the first group makes 20 to 40 percent fewer mistakes than the second group. It just proves that if you

Kanoe Durdan Spear and Quick Rush competing in youth working cowhorse in a Roseburg, Ore., Quarter Horse show. **Photo by Rabinsky**

tell someone he's dumb, he will make dumb mistakes.

It's the same in horse training. If you get on a horse every day and think, "This dumb ol' potlicker is worthless," he probably will be. But if you get on him with a more realistic attitude such as, "You're not the most talented horse in the world, but you'll make someone a terrific trail-riding horse," he will. Your attitude is reflected in how you work with him. You have to find something positive about every horse and build on that. If you have a totally defeated attitude about a horse, he *will* be worthless.

You have to apply the same philosophy to riders. One time I was judging a show with Charley Araujo, one of the all-time great horsemen. In one class he judged, a little girl had nothing but grief . . . she couldn't get anything done with her horse. But as he went down the line-up of horses, Charley told her something like, "You have a real pretty horse and he has a super walk."

One of my students for ten years, Ann Marie Monson is shown competing in a trail class at Santa Barbara, Calif., on Mizzy. In 24 shows one year, Ann Marie and Mizzy won 12 all-arounds and 11 reserve all-arounds. Ann Marie lives in Kent, Washington.

Photo by Fallaw

When I commented how surprised I was that he found something good to say about her, he replied, "That's the key to helping riders. You can always find something good to say about them, and that will encourage them to go on and try even harder."

I've learned how very true that is. But you've got to be honest with people. If a rider really has a terrible go, you can't tell him he was terrific . . . he'll know you're not telling the truth. But there will always be something he did well.

To wrap this up, here are several thoughts.

1/ Before riding your horse through the gate, always have a game plan in mind and know exactly what you are going to do, and when you are going to do it. If it's a western riding class, know exactly where you will make your changes. If it's a reining class, ride the pattern several times in your mind, mentally reviewing the process for asking for stops, lead changes, and so forth. And know exactly where you will make your circles, lead changes, and stops. It also helps to walk the pattern on foot, in the arena, during the lunch break, or before the show starts.

2/ Don't let other riders psych you out. Some riders will deliberately do this, or some will unintentionally do it, by telling you something like, "The far corner is sure spooking the horses," or "The footing is too deep for the horses to stop well," or. . . .

When you hear comments like this, your mind starts worrying: "Gosh, I'm afraid my horse will spook," or, "He's not gonna be able to stop." Wipe out those negative thoughts and think positively: "My horse never shies and he won't start now," and "He's such a good horse, he'll find a way to stop."

3/ If you have trouble handling the pressure of showing, set up little contests with yourself, and with other riders. Over the years, I set up a lot of pressure situations when I was giving lessons. Suppose, for example, Susie could make her horse change leads perfectly at home, but was always blowing them at a show. I'd tell her, "If you don't get all your lead changes right this afternoon, you have to buy all the kids a Coke." That put her in a pressure situation, and she learned to handle it better.

You can do the same thing by yourself. Say, "Self, if you don't do your lead changes right, or if you can't make these walk-overs perfectly, you can't have any dessert tonight."

One time I had a rider who always let herself get distracted in the show ring. So at home, while she was going through the trail course or whatever, I would have several kids out there banging on trash cans, hollering at her, playing the radio real loud . . . until she learned to block out those distractions.

4/ Suppose you go to a show and your horse blows the first class. All too often the tendency is to start making excuses and thinking you might as well go home. The trick here is to learn from your mistakes; determine why the horse blew the class and work to correct it. We can all learn from our mistakes, and then we will be better riders. Never let your attitude defeat you. I always tell my riders that classes in a horse show are like innings in a baseball game; each one is different, and one shouldn't have anything to do with another.

One of my students, Pandi Honald, won about 40 all-arounds during her youth career. To have a shot at winning an all-around, most kids figure they must win the showmanship, always one of the first classes at a show. Pandi did win a lot of showmanship classes, but if she didn't, she never let it rattle her.

She always said that the easiest classes to win are those toward the end of the show when other youngsters are getting tired and bored, and have lost the incentive to win.

5/ There is a wide variety of instructional videotapes on the market today, and they are an excellent tool for learning. Watching a videotape is almost like a private lesson every time you watch it. Furthermore, you are more relaxed while watching it than you might be during an actual lesson, and people absorb a lot more when they are relaxed.

If you watch a tape frequently enough, pretty soon your subconscious takes over and when you get on your horse, you will be making the same moves with the same timing and rhythm that you saw on the tapes.

Many riders and trainers also have themselves videotaped while schooling or showing to see where they are making mistakes. This is an excellent idea, but do *not* watch your mistakes over and over. Just as your subconscious can absorb the right way to do something, it can also absorb the wrong way. Study the tape to see how and why you made a mistake, but then go on. Concentrate on the positive.

SETTING GOALS

I think anyone who is serious about showing horses should have a goal foremost in his mind. Otherwise, it's like a ship sailing from port with no specific destination; it just wanders aimlessly about the ocean. With a goal in mind, accomplishments come so much easier because you will apply yourself more diligently.

It doesn't have to be a major goal, such as winning a world championship; it could be simply to do well in the county 4-H horse show; or to have your young horse well-broke by the end of summer.

It doesn't have to be one goal, it could be a series of goals. Set the first goals small, and then go up one peg at a time. That's how many great riders develop. They set a goal of first doing well in local shows, then state shows, then on a national level. In some fields of riding, that can lead to world competition.

In my experience, those who say they just show for fun never really get anywhere and plateau out, ending up as "vanilla" competitors and never winning anything. That can become discouraging for anyone—including someone who just shows for fun.

But I'm not saying everyone who rides should set a goal of becoming a world-class competitor because I realize many people have no interest in showing. On the other hand, some people who ride strictly for pleasure could benefit by becoming better riders, and a goal in that direction would help.

It could be goals such as learning to ride without bouncing in the saddle, or without bumping the horse in the mouth, or learning what leads are and how to teach the horse to take the correct leads. This is where some of the exercises discussed in Chapter 15 can play a role, because they will help accomplish those goals.

You could even set a series of goals. For example, you can declare, "In 30 days I will know how to laterally control my horse. In 60 days, I will know how to make him take the correct leads. In 90 days, I will know how to make him change leads while going over a low jump. And in 120 days, I will be able to make him do a flying change of leads every six strides."

Even if you never plan to show a horse, setting goals will help you become a better rider which, in turn, will make you enjoy riding even more. And the better rider you are, the more your horse will enjoy you!

17 WHAT TO WEAR

One thing I really like to see on a rider is a good hat that's properly blocked.

Most judges like to see a tailored, conservative outfit that fits well and looks good. This fitted shirt worn by Jill Shrake has a checkered suede yoke.

Most judges are good horsemen and can often tell if a rider is a good horseman simply by what he wears and the equipment he uses. If you *look* like a good rider, you make a favorable impression on the judge as soon as you walk into the arena.

Because most judges also tend to be conservative, a gaudy outfit with sequins and fringe is likely to turn a judge off. What most judges like to see is a tailored, conservative outfit that fits well and looks good. Having the "right look" usually doesn't cost that much more, and will pay off in a better appearance.

Taking the time to select clothes that enhance your appearance and make you feel good can be a great confidence-builder. So can the right colors. While the color(s) of your outfit should complement the horse, I think it's just as important to choose a color that makes you feel good. Almost everyone has a favorite color, and if you are wearing it when you show, you will do a better job of riding. It's psychological.

One thing I really like to see on a rider is a good hat that's properly blocked, and not a $3.98 felt from a discount store. Your hat can make or break the image you are trying to give of being a top hand. Hats should also be of the current popular style, and not one that faded into obscurity five years ago.

Good chaps that fit properly are also important in creating the right look. The best ones are usually made of ultrasuede or some type of cowhide. Naugahyde chaps simply do not look good in the show ring. Two advantages of ultra-suede: 1) This material is available in a wide range of colors, making it easy to match or complement other colors in your outfit, and 2) It washes great, making it easy to keep ultrasuede chaps clean.

There are two different types of chaps, batwings and shotguns, but the latter are preferred for almost all show-ring events. The exception is cutting, in which batwings are the most popular.

Make sure your chaps fit properly. Most chaps bought "off the shelf" will not, and some custom chapmakers do not understand that show-ring chaps should fit differently than chaps for ranch work or everyday riding. A good chapmaker also understands that show-

Few judges would ever object to jeans worn under chaps in a horsemanship class.

Shannon Baker's outfit is excellent for horsemanship classes. Note that her chaps are scalloped instead of fringed, and that her gloves are the same color as her sleeves; this minimizes the appearance of any hand movement. **Photo by Steve White**

121

These chaps worn by Angie Ross are an excellent example of how show-ring chaps should fit.

Ponytails are okay as long as they are short (so they do not bounce) and hang straight down the middle. The judge likes to see a straight line from the center of the head down the back to the center of the cantle. A ponytail hanging off to one side like this throws that line out of kilter.

ring chaps are cut longer than other chaps so they cover the heels. However, they shouldn't hang too low because that extra length will swing back and forth, giving the impression that it's your legs swinging back and forth.

If you are worried about the cost of custom chaps, remember that good ones will last for years—and you can wear jeans under them, thereby avoiding the cost of custom-tailored dress pants. I doubt if any judge objects to well-fitted jeans on an equitation rider.

As already mentioned, wearing a favorite color gives a psychological boost, but colors can also help in other ways. For example, darker colors such as navy blue, rust, and even black can make an overweight rider appear slimmer. Light colors, on the other hand, add bulk to extra-thin riders—and so do horizontal stripes. But vertical stripes give the impression of slimness.

Since light colors accentuate movement, white chaps or any light-color chaps should not be worn (especially on a dark horse) unless you can keep your legs very quiet. For the same reason, white gloves should be avoided. Gloves are not worn as frequently as in years past . . . they seem to be another old tradition getting lost. If you do wear them, however, they should match or blend with the color of your sleeves. A distinct color contrast between gloves and sleeves accentuates any movement of your hands.

Belts are necessary, of course, and are worn with some type of trophy buckle that's either been won or purchased. The color of your belt should match or blend with the other colors in your outfit.

A shirttail that has worked its way out can detract from your appearance, so take whatever steps are necessary to prevent this problem. Some riders have shirts custom-made with extra-long tails.

A simple scarf tie worn around the neck or under the collar adds a nice finishing touch for both boys and girls, but it shouldn't be so long that it flaps in the wind. Girls often add a silver pin or concha to their scarf ties. These ties come in a wide range of colors, making it easy to find one for almost any outfit.

Earrings should not be the dangling type because they give the impression that your head is moving. Besides, they just aren't appropriate for the show ring. Something else that both boys and girls should avoid is feathers in a hatband; they detract from the conservative appearance generally expected in an equitation class.

This chapter is just a brief treatise on clothes, partly because fashions and styles change, and more specific information given here might be outdated five years after this book is published. For more ideas on what to wear in the show ring, visit some shows and study what riders are currently wearing. If you have a height or weight problem, talk to someone knowledgeable who can help you choose colors and styles that will help mask your particular problem and enhance your appearance in the show ring.

Fringe on chaps should come down the back of the leg, as it does on Dameron Allen's chaps.

123

18 GROOMING

There are three basic essentials to a healthy coat.

Holy Toledo! That's probably what an old-timer would exclaim if he watched horses being prepared for the show ring today. He would see them being pampered with such products as conditioning shampoos, hot-oil treatments, mane and tail texturizers, protein hoof treatments, and all kinds of sprays to add luster and sheen to the coat.

In the old days, we'd just catch a horse out of pasture, brush him off real good, and he was ready to be shown. But to be competitive today, a horse must look like a million bucks.

I'll tell you what though, despite all the grooming products on the market, you still can't make a silk purse out of a sow's ear. In other words, if a horse doesn't have a good healthy coat, applying gallons of SuperDuper Show Shine the day before the show won't do much good.

There are three basic essentials to a healthy coat, and they have to be practiced year-round, not just during the show season. They are: 1) A good nutritional program, 2) A regular deworming program, and 3) A regular grooming program that includes lots of elbow grease.

A judge's eye is always attracted to a well-groomed horse, such as Dameron Allen's Appaloosa mare, Mighty Misty Blue.

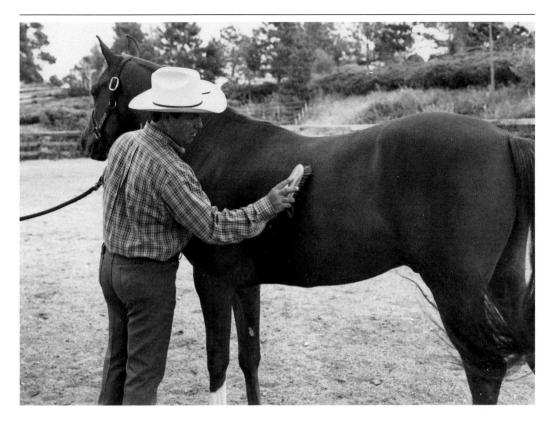

After I go over the horse with a small rubber curry, I use a stiff brush on the body to flick out dust and dirt. I use a softer brush on the head and legs.

Everyone has his own idea about which feeds to use, and my personal choice has always been whole oats and quality alfalfa hay. The hay should be green and leafy, and free of mold and dust. When I was operating Horsemanship West, I also liked to have the horses fed three times a day, at regular times. Oregon State University conducted some frequency-of-feeding tests which revealed that horses fed three times a day, at the exact same times each day, did better than horses fed once a day or twice a day.

So it's a proven fact that horses kept in stalls or corrals do better and are happier when fed small amounts several times a day, rather than a huge amount once a day. In their natural state, horses are free-roaming animals accustomed to grazing at their leisure all day and night. And their digestive system is also designed to handle this type of feeding; i.e., small amounts consumed frequently. This means fewer chances for digestive problems such as colic to develop.

Feeding several times a day also reduces the hours of boredom for confined horses. And because horses are creatures of habit, they like to be fed on time. I found that when we were trying to put weight on horses, we were a lot more

successful when we fed at the exact same times every day. If a horse is accustomed to his morning feeding at, say, 7 a.m., he gets restless and frustrated if he has to wait until 8 or 9. And then, because he's so hungry, he might bolt his feed, which can lead to colic.

Most horsemen are aware of the importance of regular deworming, not only for good health, but also to minimize the chance of colic. Be aware, though, that a horse with internal parasites can still have a nice-looking coat. So just because a horse is fat and healthy looking doesn't mean he is worm-free.

How often to deworm depends on each individual situation. For example, a few horses grazing a 1,000-acre pasture do not need worming as frequently as 30 horses kept in a 5-acre pasture, or horses kept in stalls or pens. So talk to your vet about the best program for your horses.

Once you have established a good horse management program, daily grooming is the third key to producing a coat that literally glistens in the sunlight. This is where the elbow grease fits in! My favorite grooming tool is a small rubber curry that I use in long, even strokes with the hair, not against it. If you use this hard every day, it pushes out the dirt, and I believe it also helps firm up or tone the muscles. But you

To help the mane lie flat, a damp towel works well.

This Arabian gelding, Bask Kaleed, has been closely trimmed around his muzzle, under the jaw, and at the ears, and shows the longer bridle-path and mane typical of Arabians. He was owned by Vickey Bowman of Salt Lake City when we took these pictures; he is now owned by Jackie Robel of Scottsdale, Arizona.

have to push hard, and that's what I mean by elbow grease.

I don't use the curry in a circular motion because that can break or damage the hairs. The goal is a coat that lies flat, and currying with the hair helps produce this. Next, I go all over the horse's body with a stiff brush, using it vigorously to flick out any dirt. Again, I brush with the hairs, not against them. Finally, I use a soft brush on the head and legs.

It's sort of pointless to spend a lot of time currying and brushing if the horse is dirty or sweaty, so I wash him as often as necessary to keep him clean. Some

horsemen say that frequent washing removes the natural oils from the coat, but I don't believe that's true. As proof, many men and women who have beautiful, healthy hair wash it as frequently as every day.

I've also found that if a horse has a winter coat, washing him in warm water every day in the spring will make him shed out faster than almost anything else.

To help keep a short haircoat on horses in the winter, I always blanket them—and I keep sheets on them during the summer not only to protect the coat, but also to protect the horse from flies and other insects. Of course, blankets and sheets should be kept clean—to help keep the haircoat clean.

Because today's western show horse needs a long, full tail, we keep the tails braided and tied up. This prevents tail hairs from getting snagged and pulled out, or from simply being swished out. However, this practice is only recommended for horses kept in stalls. Why? If a horse is in a corral or pasture and snags his braided tail on something, he could jerk a huge chunk of tail out. It has happened. Besides, outside horses need their tails for insect protection, and if they're braided up, they're pretty useless.

The day before a show, we like to trim the horses with clippers. We start by clipping the muzzle hairs, using a No. 40 blade, which trims much closer than the standard No. 10 blade. Next, we trim off the long hairs around the eyes . . . because this makes the eyes look larger and more expressive.

A lot of people don't like to clip the inside of the ears, because those hairs help keep insects out of the ears. I don't blame them, especially if their horses are not kept in stalls and protected from flies. But if you're going to be competitive in the show ring, you almost have to clean out those ears.

We use the No. 40 blade on the ears, being careful to hold the ear out to the side so the clipped hairs fall to the outside and not into the ear. Use long, even strokes with the clippers for a smooth-looking job. After trimming the ears, I like to take some cotton moistened with alcohol to swab out the ears. This cleans out any dirt and clipped hairs.

How long to trim the bridlepath depends on the individual horse and the breed style. Many Arabians have a bridlepath 12 inches long or longer, but Quarter Horses, Paints, Appaloosas, and similar horses have much shorter bridlepaths. I personally think that a two- to four-inch bridlepath is about right for the average horse. But if a horse has a short, thick neck, a longer bridlepath can give the neck the illusion of looking longer.

For trimming off the fetlock hairs and around the coronet band, I switch to the No. 10 blade, and am careful to clip with the hair to make everything look smooth. If a horse has white socks, I also keep them clipped because then they are easier to keep clean.

We always try to wash a horse the day before a show, partly to save time, but also to allow the coat time to flatten. This is especially true if the horse has any length to his coat. After being washed, the hairs tend to fluff up, but after being blanketed overnight, they will flatten out nicely.

On the day of the show, we add the finishing touches. I like to use a little vaseline on the muzzle and around the eyes to bring out the highlights, and some type of coat conditioner to add sheen to the coat. Of course, fly spray is essential for outdoor shows during the insect season.

Hoofs should be washed and clean, and you can use a hoof black on the dark hoofs, and a clear polish on the light-colored hoofs. I've noticed, however, that more and more exhibitors today aren't using anything on the hoofs other than a natural, clear conditioner, and I don't think any judge would object to that.

Sanding down the hoofs is one thing that any horseshoer will tell you should *never* be done. This practice got started in the Arabian breed and still persists. Each hoof is sanded to a smooth finish, then a hoof polish is applied. Repeated sandings destroy the periople and hoof wall. This can lead to quarter cracks, bruises, abcesses, and no place in which to place nails when shoeing the horse.

After a last-minute polish with a soft towel, the horse is ready. It's a lot of work to have him looking his finest, but it will pay off . . . you can bet on it!

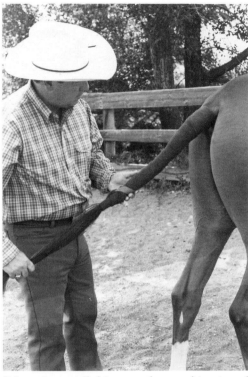

Wrapping a tail this way after washing it and just before a class helps to "control" it, and will also protect it during hauling. Be very careful not to wrap a tail too tight, however. This restricts the circulation and can result in the tail falling off, literally.

Sanding down the hoofs is one thing that any horseshoer will tell you should never be done.

We like to keep tails braided and tied up to prevent the hairs from getting swished out or snagged and pulled out. But this practice is only recommended for horses kept in stalls.

19 SAFETY

It's amazing how often a gentle horse will get you hurt.

Whether you are a raw beginner or a seasoned professional, always keep safety foremost in mind when working with or around horses. This includes *all* horses, even the ones that are dog gentle. As many a horseman will tell you, it's amazing how often a gentle horse will get you hurt, because he lulls you into a false sense of security and you forget the rules of safety.

On the other hand, when you expect trouble with a horse, you remain alert and cautious—and if the expected does happen, you often escape unhurt.

Since it would require volumes of space to cover the subject of safety completely, we can only offer a brief treatise here, but we hope that the information helps both you and your horse avoid accidents.

Tying. If statistics were kept regarding how many horses have been killed or injured in tying accidents, it would boggle our minds. Not to be overlooked are the people injured while trying to untie a struggling horse, or who get in the path of a horse that's broken loose, or . . . . The possibilities are endless.

1/ Always tie with a stout halter and stout lead rope. The good ones cost

The cardinal rule for tying: Always tie short and high (above the horse's eye level). Also use a stout halter and lead rope. Tying a horse with so much slack that he can get a foot over the rope will usually result in him getting hurt.

When riding single file on a trail, keep a reasonable distance between your horse and the one in front of you. Tail-gating is an invitation to be kicked.

more money than the cheap ones, but consider them an investment in the continuing good health of your horse. If a horse fights being tied and the halter or rope breaks, he might flip over backwards, seriously injuring or killing himself. If this doesn't happen but he starts running, there's no telling where he might go or what might happen, but you can bet that the end result will probably be bad . . . especially if he runs through a barbed wire fence, or gets on a highway.

2/ Use caution regarding the footing where you tie a horse, especially if you think he might pull back. In such a case, never tie on concrete or slippery footing because he can get hurt if his feet go out from under him.

3/ Always tie to something solid and secure that the horse cannot break, and that will not move. For example, when tying to a fence, tie to a post, not a board. There are horror stories about horses that have been tied to boards; if a horse pulls back, the board comes loose, the horse is still tied to it, he gets scared and starts running. If this happens in a crowded arena, look out!

Accidents have also happened to horses tied to movable objects, such as a big trash dumpster, or a horse trailer not attached to a vehicle or braced so it can't roll. If the horse should happen to pull back and the object moves a little, it will scare him; he pulls back harder, it begins moving faster, and . . . .

4/ Always tie a horse at the level of his eyes, or higher. If he's tied low and pulls back, he can pull his neck down. This is a permanent injury that might render him useless for the rest of his life, and it sometimes happens to foals being taught to stand tied.

Leading. The correct way to lead a horse is to walk alongside his head, with the hand closest to the horse holding the lead rope near the halter, and the balance of the lead rope in the other hand. Most people lead from the left side of the horse, but there's no reason you can't lead from the right side. In fact, a horse should lead from either side, and it's surprising how many won't lead when the handler is on the right side.

129

If you don't have a keeper for your tie-down strap, the horse could easily get a foot over it when he drops his head to graze or drink. Refer to the chapter on equipment to see how the keeper can be attached to the breast collar.

When you are leading a horse in the correct position, you are better able to control him if he suddenly jumps or tries to bolt. If, on the other hand, you are walking in front of him and something boogers him from the rear, he might jump on top of you.

Use caution in how you carry the excess lead rope. *Never* wrap it around your hand or arm, or put your hand through the coils. If the horse were to suddenly jump, those coils could tighten up and trap your hand—and if he were to start running, you could be dragged. Always hold the excess lead rope or longe line so you can immediately drop it if necessary.

This brings up a special warning to youngsters: *Never tie a lead rope or longe line around your body.* Kids will sometimes do this, believing it will help them hold a horse if he tries to get away. Sadly, several youngsters have been dragged to death as a result. It should not be done with any horse, not even a well-broke, gentle kids' horse.

You can never tell when something might startle any horse. If he jumps and jerks you down, that will scare him and he will start running. The more he runs, the more scared he gets by your being dragged along.

We know of a youngster who was riding a horse and was dragged to death after she fell off. Apparently she had tied a lead rope around her waist so that if she did fall off, the horse couldn't get away. When she did fall, the terror-stricken horse began running, and by the time passers-by could get him stopped, the child was dead.

There is no way that even Rambo can hold a horse that bolts and runs. It's much safer to drop everything in a hurry and let him go, because a horse's safety is never worth the price of a human life.

Halters. This is a special tip for the safety of horses: Never leave a halter on a loose horse. This applies regardless of where a horse is: in a box stall, corral, the front yard, or a 10,000-acre pasture. Halters are death traps if they hang up on something like a fence post, door latch, water hydrant, tree branch, etc. A horse can even get a hind foot hung up in a halter when he tries to scratch an ear. Every year, a number of horses are seriously injured or killed as a result of halter accidents.

Catch ropes or lariats. While a catch rope can be a useful tool, it can also be a death trap. It's for this reason that some 4-H horse club rules, and rules of other youth organizations, do not allow youngsters to carry a rope or reata.

Years ago, former WH Editor Chuck King wrote an article called "Safety With a Rope" (April '67). In it he points out that the job of a rope "is to catch and hold, and it can catch a rider as well as an animal." For example, if you have a rope secured to your saddle and your horse bucks you off, you can hang up a spur or even a boot in the rope coils and be dragged. This is even more apt to happen if the rope is tied to the rear saddle strings rather than on the fork. (In fact, this can happen if you have a halter and lead rope tied behind the cantle.)

1/ If you must carry a rope, secure it to the saddle with the rope strap on the fork; never carry it tied to the saddle horn. For added safety, some cowboys cut the rope strap halfway through so if they do hang up, the strap will break.

2/ Never play around with a rope by roping other riders or their horses. You never know when a rope might spook a horse, causing him to stampede. If you're tied on, you're in for a serious wreck. Or if you rope another rider and your horse stampedes, that rider can be killed.

This is only a quick look at the dangers involved with ropes. Just keep in mind that a rope is not a play toy; it can be a deadly weapon. If you are serious about learning to rope, have someone knowledgeable teach you all the safety do's and don'ts.

Horseplay. Lots of youngsters, as well as adults, sometimes get to playing around on horses—such as trying to pull a rider off his horse, or trying to get him

Hay nets should always be tied high so a horse can't get a foot in them.

bucked off. Even though it's just in fun, all too often someone gets hurt. Roughhousing around horses can also be risky; even a dog-gentle horse can get spooked by this and hurt someone. The moral of this advice: When you want to play and have fun, leave your horses in the barn!

Equipment. Good equipment is a good investment in safety. Things made cheaply are more apt to break, and when a piece of equipment on a horse breaks, the consequences can be serious. Likewise, equipment must be kept in good shape; this means regular cleaning and saddle-soaping, and replacing worn-out parts. Here are some tips:

1/ If your saddle has a back cinch, keep it snug against the belly. It's not unusual to see a back cinch hanging up to eight inches below the belly. Not only does this make the back cinch useless, it's dangerous. If a horse kicks at a fly, for example, he can catch a back foot in the cinch, and then things really get western. Or, he can also stick a back foot in it when crossing water—when horses tend to pick their back feet up higher. This

When longeing a horse, keep the excess line coiled neatly, with your hand around the coils, not in them. Then you can immediately drop them if necessary and not get your hand trapped. Letting the excess line lie around your feet can get a foot trapped.

has happened, and has sent the riders to the hospital.

A loose back cinch can also get hung up on brush or other objects in rough country.

2/ There should be a connecting strap between the front and back cinches; it prevents the back cinch from slipping too far back into the flanks and possibly causing the horse to buck. For safety's sake, there should be no slack in the connecting strap so it doesn't snag any brush, etc.

3/ Always remember when unsaddling to unbuckle the back cinch first, and then the front cinch. See the chapter on saddling for more details.

4/ If you ride with a tie-down, it should have a keeper of some sort, which is attached to the breast collar. Without this keeper, the horse can easily get a foot over the tie-down when he puts his head down to graze or drink.

5/ Never attach the tie-down to the curb strap or curb chain! It seems ridiculous to mention this, but some riders have been seen with the tie-down attached in this manner. This makes the bit virtually useless and can result in the horse getting out of control . . . not to mention the fact he jerks his mouth every time he raises his head.

6/ Snaps on reins are handy, but dangerous as they can easily come unsnapped all by themselves—and usually at the worst possible time such as when you are merrily galloping along. It's much safer to secure reins to the bit with leather tie thongs.

7/ Chicago screws fall into the same category as snaps. Many bridles have these screws, and it's not unusual for the bit to fall out of the horse's mouth when one of those screws works loose—again, at the most inopportune times. If your bridle does have these screws, coating them with clear nail polish makes them far less likely to work loose.

Rider's gear. It is an ironclad rule that one should always wear boots when riding a horse, yet this rule is ignored by thousands of riders who much prefer to ride in tennis shoes or other types of athletic shoes. They are dangerous because they do not have heels. Should you be wearing tennies and get in a storm with your horse, a foot could slip all the way through the stirrup and you could be dragged. Some riders have been dragged to death.

Heels on boots greatly lessen the chance of a boot slipping through the stirrup, and the old-style undershot heels make it practically impossible.

If you value your life and limb, *always* wear boots when riding, and do not be influenced by others wearing tennies. In fact, you should also wear boots or good leather shoes whenever working around horses simply for the protection they provide should ol' Bay step on your foot.

The other safety item that *all* riders should consider using is a safety helmet. Each year, a number of riders are killed as a result of head injuries suffered in a fall from a horse. Safety helmets are required in practically all hunter and jumper events, but thus far have been shunned by western riders because they are not stylish. Then, too, many western horse show rules require that a western hat be worn. This may change in time, especially in the speed and working events when a fall is more apt to occur. In fact, effective in January 1987, AQHA rules now allow riders in any class to wear a hard hat or safety helmet.

Also, give serious thought to wearing a protective helmet when riding at home, especially when doing such things as breaking a colt, running barrels, etc.

On the Trails. There are a host of rules that trail riders should observe, not only

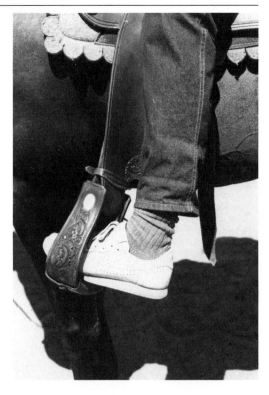

Riding in tennies or other athletic shoes is an absolute no-no because it's an invitation to big trouble.

for their own safety, but for that of fellow riders.

1/ Never crowd the horse in front of you when riding single-file. Many horses object to tail-gaters and will kick.

2/ If a rider must dismount for whatever reason, other riders should wait until that rider is safely back in the saddle. Many horses will not stand quietly to be mounted if their buddies are leaving, and this could spell trouble for the rider trying to get on such a horse.

3/ Do not trot or lope by other horses, unless you are absolutely positive it will not upset those horses. Some horses get excited when a galloping horse roars by and will try to join in the fun. If their riders are not skilled enough to control them or stay on, an accident can result.

4/ If you are riding at the head of the group, keep an eye on the end of the line and stop when necessary for the tail-enders to catch up.

All riders should consider using a safety helmet, or hard hat.

133

Here's the proper way to lead a horse. Keep the excess lead rope coiled neatly so you can drop it quickly and not get your hand trapped if the horse bolts suddenly.

Most people lead from the left side of the horse, but there's no reason you can't lead from the right side.

5/ Likewise, if you are riding at the tail end, make an effort to stay up with the rest of the group.

6/ A large group of riders should appoint a drag rider, who rides at the end of the line and makes sure that no riders are lost or left behind.

7/ Never ground-tie a horse on the trail. As the old saying goes, "A ground-tied horse is a loose horse," and you might have a long walk home if he takes off. Some horses ground-tied on mountain trails have galloped off, not to be found for several days. And sometimes the saddles they were packing were never found. If you know you will be stopping along the trail and will need to tie up, leave a halter under the bridle and carry along a lead rope.

8/ Do not tie with the bridle reins because they easily break if a horse pulls back.

9/ When descending a steep bank, keep the horse pointed straight down. Then if he starts to slide, he will slide straight down with no problem. But if he's angled sideways and starts to slide, he could lose his balance.

10/ When going up steep hills, it's easier on the horses to zig-zag back and forth rather than heading straight up.

11/ When crossing a stream or river, never look down at the water. This can mesmerize a rider, causing him/her to topple off into the water.

12/ Do not assume that all horses can automatically swim; some can't, and have drowned as a result of being ridden into deep water.

13/ When crossing deep water, remove your tie-down because a horse can't swim if his head is tied down. Also make sure your back cinch is tight so the horse won't stick a hind foot through it.

14/ If your horse starts swimming and you get off, always stay behind him or to the side. If you get in front of him, he might "climb" right up on top of you.

15/ If you must lead a horse down a steep slope, try to stay to one side. If you are directly in front of him, he might slide or stumble into you.

It's safest to use tie thongs on bridle reins, not snaps.

16/ If you dismount to lead a reluctant horse across a narrow stream, stand to one side after you get across. Otherwise he might leap right on top of you.

17/ If you see a thunderstorm approaching and you are above timberline or in a wide-open area, get out of there as fast as possible. Head for a valley or a more sheltered area where you will not be such an inviting target for lightning.

18/ If you are not sure if your horse is slicker broke, dismount to put it on.

19/ Use a breast collar when riding in steep country to help keep your saddle from sliding back. Adjust it carefully, though, so it doesn't ride too high and cut off the horse's wind. For trail riding, many people prefer the mohair-type breast collars, rather than leather, because mohair is cooler and will not gall a horse.

20/ If your saddle tends to slip forward when you are going downhill, you might need a crupper. This is standard equipment on most mules, but some horses need a crupper, too.

21/ If your horse kicks at other horses, tie a red ribbon in his tail as a warning to other riders to "stay clear."

PROFILE: RICHARD SHRAKE

Richard and his wife, Lee Ann.

Although he was raised on a farm with horses and showed them as a teenager, Richard Shrake had no idea of making a career in the horse business. Nor did he have any inkling that he would become one of the nation's top trainers, instructors, and judges, who would also be giving clinics all over the nation.

"When I graduated from high school," he remembers, "I didn't know what I wanted to do. I just went off to college like everybody else, and started out in animal science like all the other kids raised on farms and ranches. Later, I switched to education because I thought I could keep up my grade-point average a little easier . . . I was not well equipped for nuclear physics," he laughs. "And I graduated with a degree in education."

Nevertheless, his experience with horses as a youth had already laid the foundation for what was to become his life's work.

Richard was born in 1944 in Salem, Ore., the son of Warren and Eva Shrake, who operated a dairy farm. "But my dad had always loved horses. He was raised in Colorado and did a lot of rodeoing in his younger days, and was a member of the old Cowboys Turtle Association (forerunner of the Professional Rodeo Cowboys Association).

"We always had all kinds of horses on the farm, and not necessarily registered ones. Dad did a lot of trading, and that gave my brother, Greg, and me plenty of experience with different horses and colts and getting them broke well

A 1986 photo of the Shrakes' youngsters: Joey (left), Justin, and Jill.

enough to trade 'em off."

When Richard was about nine years old, the family went to the county fair, and he took along a pony his dad had given to him. "I kinda watched the kids competing in showmanship and horsemanship. I thought, 'That looks like fun.' Not only did I show my pony successfully, I got a good offer to sell him because he did so well."

Richard proved to be a quick study. "The only reason I did well is because I carefully watched the other kids. Whatever they did, I did, and I finished the day as champion showman in my age division."

That sparked an interest in showing that continues to this day. "I was lucky because we belonged to the Salem Saddle Club, headquartered at the Oregon State Fairgrounds, and through the club's activities, there were many opportunities to learn. The club was always putting on horse shows and clinics, which gave us the chance to be around some really good horsemen.

"For example, for three winters I took lessons from a German dressage trainer. I really wasn't that thrilled about dressage, to be real honest, but he was the only trainer I could afford to work with. And what I learned from him has benefitted me throughout my career.

Lee Ann, Jill, and Richard at the '79 Quarter Horse Congress where both Jill and Richard won all-arounds. **Photo by Harold Campton**

"The club also had a number of adult members who always had time to work with us kids and teach us more about horses. It was a great experience."

Richard was not the only youngster from that club who went on to make a mark in the horse world. Two of his buddies included Larry Mahan, who went on to win umpteen bronc riding, bull riding, and all-around championships in professional rodeo, and Doug Brown, who became a world champion bull rider.

Richard rode his own horse, Hasty Amigo, to win the title of grand champion working horse, junior riders, at the 1961 Redmond Horse Show. **Photo by Rabinsky**

Throughout his teen-age years, Richard continued competing in open shows, which were tremendously popular at that time, as well as at some AQHA shows in which he won a couple of all-arounds. That so excited him that he became more enthusiastic than ever about showing.

"When it was time for college, I went to Oregon State University because it had a pretty good riding program, but I wasn't thinking I wanted to get into the horse business. I did take a couple of horses to college with me, however. These were horses that I was training for other people to earn some extra money. I did that for all four years, and it truly helped me get through school."

Although Richard started college at OSU, he later transferred to Portland State, and that's where he earned his degree in education. One might think a major in education would be of little help to someone who would make a

career with horses, but Richard doesn't feel that way. "Those courses were terrific because they helped me to learn how to deal with people, taught me about business, and gave me a good education in something besides horses."

Richard says he got two lucky breaks after college that steered him into a career with horses. The first was a job with the Circle W Ranches in Oregon City, owned by Ben and Lois Weiler. Says Richard, "I had been showing a Morgan in hackamore classes, and he was a stoppin', turning-around machine. I won quite a few classes with him. Mrs. Weiler had seen me show him and was so impressed by how light this horse was and how well he worked that she and Ben hired me as their trainer in the summertime.

"Well, that led into working with their son and showing horses on the road. That job really helped me by letting me have so many nice horses to show, which in turn helped me start to make a name here in the Northwest. The Weilers were terrific people to back a 20-year-old kid."

As Richard's reputation grew, he began giving a few clinics, and this led to his second lucky break. At that time, in the 1960s, Carnation-Albers (makers of feeds and supplements like Calf Manna) was a major force on the West Coast. They sponsored a number of clinics on feeds and nutrition, and their speaker was "a dynamite guy named Pat Driscoll," Richard relates. "I was always impressed with his presentations and his dedication to horse people through his activities.

"One day he watched me give a clinic, and the idea hit him that we ought to give clinics together. He would concentrate on the nutrition and feeding, and I would concentrate on training horses.

"Next thing I knew, I was giving clinics for Carnation-Albers all the way from Vancouver, Wash., south to Del Mar, California. Those clinics helped me develop my teaching ability, and I found that I really enjoyed helping people with their horses."

Yet this created conflict within Richard, who by now had his sights set on becoming a professional trainer. "It

At a Friday night playday of the Salem Saddle Club years ago, Richard took a crack at jumping on a horse called Spin Again.
Photo by J.F. Malony

seemed to me that what I would call the *pure* horse trainers liked to stay by themselves, just training their horses. They didn't give lessons or clinics, or take on any apprentices. So I kept asking myself: 'Am I really being a horse trainer?' However, I continued doing the Carnation clinics for about three years, and I'm still doing clinics today on my own."

Richard's next move was to buy acreage outside of Oregon City—part of the greater Portland area—to establish his own training stable which he called Horsemanship West. This turned out to be a shrewd move for two reasons: 1/ It gave him a base of operations, and 2/ It paid a handsome profit when he sold a chunk of the land 18 years later. But this was not just a lucky break; Richard had planned it.

"While I was showing and giving clinics in the 1960s, I got to know a lot of the top West Coast trainers. I also learned that most of them who made any real money made it in real estate. They'd buy a place in the country to raise and train horses and later sell it for a bunch of money when the city grew out to them.

"So in 1967, I bought 18 acres outside of Oregon City for $500 down and 6 percent interest. The land was out in the boonies, but I figured the city would grow that way." Indeed it did. Horsemanship West no longer exists and in its place sprawls a shopping center. But we are getting ahead of the story.

Horsemanship West started with a 38-stall barn. Soon there was an indoor arena and another barn with 20 or so stalls. During its glory years, HW averaged about 40 horses in training, plus any number of students. "I always took a bunch of students to shows," Richard smiles. "One year at the Junior Cow Palace in San Francisco, I had 28 kids there with their horses.

"We went almost every year to the big shows in Santa Barbara and I always won the award for the trainer with the most students . . . usually I had about 24 or 26. The Good Lord blessed me because I had students like Claudia Starr, Tom St. Hilaire, Pandi Honald, John

Ryan Lee Reed was an outstanding stock horse that Richard trained and showed; here they are winning a reining at the Eugene Charity Horse Show. At one point, Richard won 17 straight reinings on this horse at West Coast shows. Ryan Lee Reed was owned by Mr. and Mrs. Bill Blacklaw of Oregon City, Oregon.
Photo by Jim Bortvedt

Link, Denise Kapler, Kanoe Durdan, Sue Broadus, Megan Laidlaw, Alicia Pershern, Sue Keenan, and Jeanne Scoggin who won championships up and down the coast. They were talented kids with tremendous ability."

While he was giving lessons, Richard also continued training and showing "because I had a goal in mind. I really wanted to earn my spurs as a rider and trainer because I think if you're gonna teach it, you ought to be able to say you've done it."

When Richard began showing in higher caliber competition, he began winning, but there were minor setbacks to keep his feet firmly planted on the ground. "When I was growing up, I had heard so much about Ronnie Richards and Don Dodge and all those other California stock horse trainers. They were like heroes . . . and I almost expected them not to be real. And then I began showing against them.

"I can remember a class at the Oregon State Fair when I beat Billy Harris, Harold Farren, and Ronnie Richards in a reining class. I'll tell you what . . . I was only 22 years old and I thought I was on top of the world. Then when we came back in the stake and I was third, that brought me back to reality. But that win proved that I could do it."

It was during the 1960s and '70s when the open western division at West Coast shows approved by the American Horse Shows Association was hotly competitive. Richard figured that if he could win national championships through the AHSA high-point year-end awards (called Horse of the Year awards), he would have his credentials as a trainer and rider to fulfill his first goal.

That he did in 1974 when he won the following Horse of the Year awards: trail horse, with Midnight Owen, owned by Aline Ray of Eugene, Ore.; western pleasure, with The Highwayman, owned by Jeanne Scoggin of Seaside, Ore.; and stock horse, with Cholliewood, also owned by Jeanne Scoggin.

"After I fulfilled that first goal," Richard says, "my next goal was to prove myself as a teacher and that, in turn, would help me accomplish my third goal: to become a better judge."

Both goals were locked up with Richard's students winning an impressive array of titles up and down the West Coast, and his becoming a judge at such shows as the All American Quarter Horse Congress, the World Championship Quarter Horse Show, the Appaloosa, Paint, and Arabian nationals, and the big open shows on the West Coast.

Richard's first big judging job came in 1971. "Frank Jordano, who managed many of the major open shows in California, called and asked me to judge at Indio. Boy, that just about blew me away because I was still a kid (27) relatively speaking. I got all puffed up because in those days you could hardly judge a bigger or more prestigious show than Indio.

"I never forgot that show because everybody said I was too young to take the job, it was too early in my career, and it would be a good way to commit harikari. But, of course, being egotistical, I took the job. It turned out to be a good lesson in life for me because, although I felt good about how I handled it, several trainers questioned me later as to how I could have picked the rider I did to win the stock seat championship when she had never won one before.

"I replied, 'Well, I thought she was the best rider I had.' Later, I began scratching my head and wondered if I had been wrong, but time proved me right when that rider, Mary Bell, went on to win many more championships. That experience taught me to stand by my convictions.

"Even after all these years, I still get excited when I walk into the ring to judge a class, because there's a challenge and excitement about finding the best horse in the class. At first, I would get discouraged because I always had a mental picture of what all horses should go like and look like. But sometimes I couldn't find those horses in a class and I would get discouraged. So I had to retool my thinking to find what I thought was the perfect horse in *each* class."

One of Richard's proudest honors is the fact he was voted one of the top three western judges for several years in a row in the 1970s by readers of *HORSES* mag-

At the 1958 Oregon State Fair, Richard won the fancy turnout class with Danielle Stender.   Photo by J.F. Malony

azine. That publication was extremely popular on the West Coast during the years of the big open shows.

If you ask Richard if there is any one person to whom he gives the most credit for helping him to become a better horseman, he pauses, and then says, "No. When I was growing up, the trainers never told you much. You could work with them and pick up some of their so-called secrets, but I later learned they really weren't secrets. They simply did not understand, and/or could not explain, some of the things they did. They just knew they worked.

"I think my success has come from being observant and from keeping an open mind. I realized long ago that you can learn something from anybody . . . like the dressage trainer I took lessons from as a kid. Not long ago I was talking with a gaited-horse trainer about keeping horses light and I picked up a little tip from him, and he's never been on a western horse. I've also learned a lot from reading books and articles . . . and the upshot is that I can't give credit to just one person for most of my knowledge because it's come from so many people.

"I also like to think that I've been open to change in my methods. I have seen some people in our industry who have

141

In 1974 Richard rode Cholliewood to win the stock horse championship at the City of Roses horse show in Portland—as well as the AHSA Stock Horse of the Year award. **Photo by Rabinsky**

only one way of doing something and it has really stifled them. Training has changed so much in recent years, and is still changing, and if you can't change to a better way of doing something, you'll be left behind."

Richard is the first to admit that some of his training methods have changed drastically since he was a kid breaking colts for his dad. "I gradually found that horses learn so much faster when no force is used. But the key is that we're working with a completely different type of horse than what we had in the 1940s and '50s, and in the years before that. Those horses were cold-blooded and didn't have much sensitivity, and sometimes not too much sense. The average horses today, like well-bred reining horses, have hotter blood and are so sensitive that you can't put the hammer down on them. Our approach today has to be a lot softer and kinder."

With the closing of Horsemanship West, Richard and his family moved from the big-city hustle of Portland over the Cascade Range to the more tranquil country of Sunriver, Oregon. Richard is married to his second wife, Lee Ann, and the family includes their son, Justin, and Lee Ann's daughters, Jill and Joey.

Although Lee Ann enjoys the horses and loves to watch the kids show, she doesn't ride, "which is kinda nice because it keeps me in touch with reality," Richard grins. "If it weren't for Lee Ann, I would probably talk, live, and breathe horses 24 hours a day. For example, when I was living next door to Horsemanship West, I might run over to check a horse on my day off, and the next thing I knew I'd been there all day. Lee Ann keeps my life in better balance."

Both girls are now in college and no longer active with horses, but did show for several years. In fact, Jill was among the last of Richard's students to become a star before Horsemanship West shut down. Among her honors, she was the high-point rider at the 1985 Junior Cow Palace in San Francisco, and won the all-around in her age division at the Quarter Horse Congress in Ohio in 1979. At that same Congress, ol' Dad, not to be outdone, showed a gray horse named Whimjammer to win the all-around.

Young Justin is tackling Sunriver Preparatory Academy right now. Richard says that Justin "has a real kindness with horses, a softness, just like my dad did, but I'm not pushing him into showing. He's really not old enough or big enough yet. I've seen too many little kids who start out showing with a bang and then get burned out real quick."

Although Richard is no longer showing, he still owns several broodmares and young horses. And he has no intention to simply lie back and enjoy life. He continues to judge at least one or two shows every month, and puts on one or two clinics every month.

"My clinics are attracting more people every year. In 1986, I estimate that about 12,000 people came as either riders or spectators. I still get a thrill out of helping people at clinics. And I feel that clinics give me the opportunity to work with so many more horsemen than I can at home on a one-to-one basis. I've also learned that there are a lot of people around the country who really love and care for their horses, but need guidance and have no place to get it because there are no trainers or instructors in the area where they live."

Even though he has been doing clinics for years, Richard says, "Every one is a thrill because I see so many people get excited when they find out they can really do something with their horses. When I receive a letter after a clinic that says, for example, "Gosh, my horse is changing leads great now and he couldn't do it before your clinic," it really makes my day because I enjoy being part of someone else's happiness."

Videotapes are another tool that Richard is using to disseminate information to horse owners. Initially, he made several tapes for the American Quarter Horse Association, including one with Clark Bradley on western horsemanship, but now he is producing his own tapes.

Over the years, Richard has also found time to give something back to the industry that has given him so much. He has served on the western committee of the AHSA, with the Professional Horsemen's Association, on various committees of his local and state Quarter Horse associations, as well as on the Governor's Youth Commission. He also coached the U.S. team against teams from Australia and Canada in a riding team competition called the World Cup.

An ebullient person who always seems to be cheerful, Richard gives a great deal of credit for his work and success to the influence of Christianity in his life. "As a child, I attended church with my parents, and have steadily grown as a Christian. Our family is a member of the Sunriver Community Church, where I also teach a youth group. We feel that Christianity is the cornerstone of our family and my profession.

"It has also allowed me to share a special fellowship with other Christian horsemen such as Al Dunning, Bob Loomis, and Doug Milholland. And it has allowed me to share some very special times with horsemen and women like the late Peggy Van Fleet who, while suffering from terminal cancer, managed to qualify her horse for the World Championship Quarter Horse Show in amateur trail and place in the top ten.

"From the very first clinic I did, it was obvious that the good Lord has given me the faith to understand what he has

At the 1979 Quarter Horse Congress, Richard won the all-around performance title on Whimjammer, owned by the E.B. Gee Ranch of Blytheville, Arkansas.   **Photo by Harold Campton**

planned for my life. I wouldn't trade it for anything."

Pat Close

IN APPRECIATION

We'd like to give a great big thanks to the riders who helped us with the majority of the photography for this book. They are:

Dameron Allen, Portland, Ore., and her Appaloosa mare, Mighty Misty Blue.

Melissa Coffey, Scappoose, Ore., and her Appaloosa gelding, Honor and Riches.

Todd Bergen, Salem, Ore., and his AQHA gelding, Docs Decision.

Kelly Holder, Canby, Ore., and her Arabian stallion, El Baraka.

Donna Martinson, Portland, Ore., and her AQHA mare, Della Do.

Angie Ross, Aurora, Colo., and her AQHA gelding, Casa String.

Jill Shrake, Sunriver, Ore., and her AQHA mare, Hobby's Diamond.

Shannon Baker, Glendale, California.

We'd also like to thank Bill and Barbara Blacklaw of Singing Hills Stables in Oregon City, and Tom and Betty Watt of Willow Springs Ranch in Colorado Springs, for letting us use their arenas for the photography sessions.

Western Horseman Magazine

Colorado Springs, Colorado

The Western Horseman Magazine, established in 1936, is the world's leading horse publication. For subscription information, write: Western Horseman Magazine, P.O. Box 7980, Colorado Springs, Colorado 80933.

Distributed to the book trade by
Texas Monthly Press, Inc.
P.O. Box 1569, Austin, TX 78767-1569
Ph. 800-288-3288